SHADOW WORK DEMYSTIFIED

A Step-by-Step Guide to Cultivate Inner Peace, Heal Deep Trauma and Emotional Triggers, and Overcome Limiting Patterns to Reclaim Your Personal Power

V. V. PHOENIX

Copyright © 2025 V. V. Phoenix. All rights reserved.

The content contained within this book may not be reproduced, duplicated, or transmitted without direct written permission from the author or the publisher.

Under no circumstances will any blame or legal responsibility be held against the publisher or author for any damages, reparation, or monetary loss due to the information contained within this book, either directly or indirectly.

Legal Notice:

This book is copyright-protected. It is only for personal use. You cannot amend, distribute, sell, use, quote, or paraphrase any part, or the content within this book, without the consent of the author or publisher.

Disclaimer Notice:

Please note that the information contained within this document is for educational and entertainment purposes only. All effort has been executed to present accurate, up-to-date, reliable, and complete information. No warranties of any kind are declared or implied. Readers acknowledge that the author is not engaged in the rendering of legal, financial, medical, or professional advice. The content within this book has been derived from various sources. Please consult a licensed professional before attempting any techniques outlined in this book.

By reading this document, the reader agrees that under no circumstances is the author responsible for any losses, direct or indirect, that are incurred as a result of the use of information contained within this document, including, but not limited to, errors, omissions, or inaccuracies.

CONTENTS

Introduction — 7

1. THE SHADOW WITHIN — 11
   The Shadow — 11
   Where Does Your Shadow Come From? — 14
   Personal vs. Collective Shadows — 15
   Shadow or Ego? — 16
   Shadow Myths—Wrecked! — 18

2. STOP RUNNING—THE SHADOW'S ALREADY IN THE ROOM — 23
   Facing the Shadow — 24
   The Cost of Avoiding Your Shadow — 28
   Shadow Work for Inner Peace — 31
   From Awareness to Strength — 32

3. SPOTTING YOUR INNER SABOTEUR — 37
   The Mirror Game — 37
   The Feelings That Reveal Your Shadow — 41
   The 3-Step Shadow Skill Drill — 43

4. BEFORE THE DIG—SETTING THE GROUND FOR INNER WORK — 45
   Building Your Inner Sanctuary — 45
   Curiosity, Not Judgment — 50
   When It Gets Uncomfortable — 51
   Becoming a Gentle Warrior — 54
   Setting Intentions — 56

5. MEETING YOUR SHADOW — 61
   Talking to What's Hidden — 61
   The Clues in Your Dreams — 67
   Shadow Journaling — 73
   Letting the Shadow Be the Artist — 77
   Calm Observation — 80

3-2-1 Shadow Process	82
The Good/Bad Box	84
6. WHEN THE GOING GETS TOUGH	87
Facing the Hard	87
Defense Mechanisms in Action	89
You Don't Have to Do This Alone	95
Keep Showing Up	96
Celebrate!	98
7. LIVING WHOLEHEARTEDLY	101
Signs That It's Working	101
What Authenticity Feels Like	104
Your Work Isn't Done	107
Share and Inspire	108
8. STEPPING INTO THE LIGHT	111
Breaking with the Old	112
Challenging a Limiting Belief	115
Using the Shadow	118
Boundaries and Choices	121
Resilience Isn't Always Loud	122
The Future You Choose	126
Conclusion	129
References	133

TRIGGER WARNING

While we won't discuss anything specific that's likely to be triggering throughout this book, you're going to be invited to look at the most uncomfortable aspects of yourself, and this may involve revisiting traumatic memories. Be kind to yourself as you embark on this journey, and do only as much as you can handle in one sitting. This is a safe place, and you're in control of your experience. If ever it feels like too much, take a break. Healing is challenging work, but it's the pathway to profound growth.

INTRODUCTION

Sometimes the hardest truths to face are the ones about ourselves. In fact, we often put a huge amount of energy into hiding them and doing everything we can to ignore them—to the extent that we don't fully know who we are.

It's almost like there are two of you inside your body. There's the conscious you, the one who gets up every morning determined to get through all your tasks and have a positive experience of the day—and then there's your shadow self. This is the unconscious part of your personality, hidden deep within, encompassing all the parts you've been inclined to ignore or bury. It involves personality traits, desires, and emotions that go against what society or the conscious version of you expects (Garoutte-Mohammed 2024). Until you get to know your shadow self, you can't fully know yourself; you're only acquainted with the part of you that meets your expectations. Growth and healing come from uniting the two—healing the wounded parts of your shadow self, then integrating it—and that's exactly what you're going to learn how to do as we move through this journey together.

As a master teacher and practitioner of Reiki and Seichim/Sekhem (energy healing modalities), and a spiritual teacher and ascension guide, I've helped many people find balance. (These may be foreign ideas to you, but I promise to lay light on the woo-woo!) I've also heard many others' personal experiences whose core wounding stems from a shadow self in desperate need of healing. What I can absolutely tell you is that it takes a huge amount of courage to admit that your shadow self is in the driver's seat, and by picking up this book, you've already taken the first step.

Perhaps you have a habit of self-sabotage. Many of the people I've worked with have had the same difficulty. They might repeatedly get in the way of their own success, whether through holding themselves to impossibly high standards, chronic procrastination, or numbing their pain with a coping mechanism that does more harm than good. They might also sabotage their relationships out of fear of losing them, resulting in exactly the outcome they wanted to avoid. Nearly always, shadow work reveals that there's more behind this issue than meets the eye; oftentimes, there's unresolved trauma or self-esteem issues that need to be addressed.

For other people, the issue is difficulty in regulating their emotions. Perhaps they're easily triggered, and this causes them to overreact in different situations, which makes it difficult for them to connect deeply with others. If this is something you struggle with, you probably find that it's affecting your relationships, and you're aware when it's happening, yet have no idea what you can do to change the situation. You might have difficulty setting boundaries, and, as a result, find yourself being taken advantage of or being overwhelmed by the amount of pressure you're under. It's also very common for people to gravitate toward relationships that mirror their past traumas or repeat unhealthy behavior patterns.

Maybe your own challenges are not as obvious. You might not think you have any issues with your relationships, but perhaps you struggle with accepting the whole authentic you. Perhaps there are parts of you that you try to hide from everyone—yourself included. If you want to change the parts of you that you don't like, you must first be brutally honest with yourself through radical self-awareness and accept them.

Whatever your personal situation is, I know something must have happened that made you fed up with the status quo. Maybe you're burnt out emotionally, or perhaps you've been through a difficult breakup that highlighted behavior patterns you're determined to let go of. Whatever happened, you're now ready to meet your whole self and work to break the cycles that have brought you here—and you will.

As we move through this book, you'll get to know yourself better and learn how to be less reactive. You'll work on breaking your destructive habits and replacing them with healthier behavior patterns. You'll learn how to access a deep sense of calm, no matter how chaotic life feels. This really is possible, and it isn't done by reading a lot of theory. My goal is to give you the practical tools you need to integrate the unconscious parts of your psyche, increase your self-awareness, regulate your emotions, and, ultimately, pave the way for personal growth. You're going to discover how to live as your most authentic self, and this is going to have a profound impact on your relationships and the level of peace and happiness you feel in your life. Don't worry, though. This isn't something you need a therapy background to understand, and it doesn't matter whether you're completely new to shadow work or you have some experience already. We're going to take it all step by step.

I'm sure a part of you is still skeptical, especially if you've been repeating the same destructive patterns for many years, but I've seen shadow work help so many people, and I know it can help you too. It's time to breathe a sigh of relief now. You're in a safe place, and you're going to learn exactly how you can embrace your whole self and reap all of the benefits that this brings. Ready? Then let's begin.

CHAPTER 1

THE SHADOW WITHIN

A study entitled *The Adverse Childhood Experiences Study*, which followed participants over many years to track the impact of childhood experiences on later life, found that 64% of participants reported at least one instance of childhood trauma. Of them, 69% experienced multiple instances (Bagga et al. 2024). These early emotional wounds don't stay in the past. They often become buried in what Swiss psychiatrist Carl Jung referred to as "the shadow" (Lonngi n.d.). The longer they're hidden, the more they shape our thoughts, feelings, and reactions—often without us even realizing it.

THE SHADOW

In simple terms, your shadow is your dark side. It's the part of your personality that's composed of natural but negative impulses and emotions like desire, greed, rage, envy, and selfishness (Jeffrey 2025a). It's all the parts of yourself you don't want to admit to, the parts that you view as being unacceptable and that may go against the grain of your conscious beliefs about yourself. It's the hidden parts of you that you've disowned. But it doesn't just contain negative aspects; it contains the seeds of your greatest power yet to be sown. Your shadow self contains all the issues that are, as yet, unresolved, the desires and passions you're not currently pursuing, and the things you want yet are just outside of your reach.

Take a moment to consider your own shadow. We have much work to do, but if you're honest with yourself, you might already have some idea of what's in there. Is it anger or people-pleasing? Maybe it's competitiveness or aggressiveness; perhaps it's sadness. Whatever you think it might be, it's okay. Your shadow isn't evil or dangerous. It's simply raw and unprocessed, and everything in there is a natural human impulse or emotion, not to be feared but to be healed and integrated.

Jung was very interested in the concept of the shadow and how to integrate it into the conscious psyche. He believed that the failure to acknowledge and address the shadow is often the root of any problem that may occur between two people or groups of people, fueling prejudice and disagreements (The Jungian Shadow 2015). This doesn't mean that there's anything bad about the shadow. He came up with the term to represent the things we're not conscious of—the things that, if we view consciousness as light, lie in its shadow (Colwell 2024). Although it is often viewed as a dark side, dark doesn't necessarily mean "bad."

You might have heard of "the collective unconscious." In Jungian theory, the personal unconscious is unique to you, but the collective unconscious is made up of memories and experiences that are shared by all humans (Sinclair n.d.). Jung described these experiences as archetypes. Eight of the most commonly discussed ones are self, shadow, anima, animus, persona, hero, wise old man, and trickster (Garoutte-Mohammed 2024):

- **Self:** This is the central archetype and the totality of your psyche.
- **Shadow:** This is the emotional part of your psyche that you may not be aware of, and the focus of our work throughout this book.
- **Anima:** This is what draws you to your feminine side.
- **Animus:** This is the masculine side of the psyche, and it's what allows you to self-reflect and understand yourself.
- **Persona:** This is the image you present to the outside world, keeping your hidden self protected.
- **Hero:** This is the part of you that's able to overcome obstacles.
- **Wise Old Man:** This is where your wisdom is held.
- **Trickster:** This is the mischievous element of your psyche that disrupts order to provoke change, having both constructive and destructive expressions.

The four main archetypes are the self, the persona, the anima/animus, and the shadow, and these are the ones we'll focus on for now (Copley 2024). The self should not be confused with the ego, however. Unlike the ego, the self includes both conscious and unconscious aspects. Jung believed that growth and development require self-realization and the ability to identify the self (Jungian Archetypes: Self, Persona, Shadow, Anima/Animus 2020). The persona, meanwhile, the mask you present to the world, reflects the roles you play throughout your life. It's important to social interactions, but it can also hide your true self; the persona can leave you feeling disconnected from the self (Copley 2024). The anima/animus, embodying the masculine and feminine elements of your psyche, affect your perception of gender, spark your intuition and creativity, and influence how you approach relationships (Copley 2024). We already know what the shadow is, and to be conscious of it, we have to put the work in. We'll delve into this more as the book goes on.

WHERE DOES YOUR SHADOW COME FROM?

When you were very young, you were taught which emotions were safe to show and which weren't. This is social conditioning, and it comes from your experiences with peers and caregivers. You were rewarded with smiles and praise when you expressed joy; you may have been punished with disappointment (or something more tangible) when you expressed anger. You were shown how to manage your emotions so that only the socially acceptable ones would be shown outwardly, and you were taught what is and isn't acceptable behavior. From this alone, you can see what may have been falling into your shadow and what was allowed into the light of your conscious self.

Not every message you received was a conscious attempt by your caregivers to program you a particular way. While they may certainly have been trying to teach you appropriate ways to behave and navigate your emotional landscape, they most likely sent out unconscious messages too. Let's say your dad really wanted you to be into football, and when you showed little interest, you saw the disappointment on his face, even though his words told you that it was okay. You might have learned to incorporate a love of football into your persona, the mask you present to the world, perhaps to the extent that you began to believe it yourself. Meanwhile, your passion for basketball, which your dad hates, might have slipped into your shadow. Every aspect of you that you were programmed to think was unacceptable was suppressed and sent to this part of your psyche. The input you received at a very young age shaped the emotional behavior you learned and how you interpret and understand your emotions (LoBue and Ogren 2021). Indeed, your early experiences, particularly with your caregivers, had a lasting impact on your emotional behavior (Gee 2020). This is closely related to the difference between your ego and your shadow. Your ego is your conscious self; your shadow, therefore, is your unconscious self.

In our football example, your enjoyment of football may have made its way into your ego, while your love of basketball slipped into the shadow. Both came from the same place, but you're not conscious of it all. Are you someone who avoids crying in front of other people? Think back to your childhood. Were you told to stop crying or conditioned to think that doing so was a sign of weakness? Then perhaps there is some part of your shadow that contains sadness, while your ego holds on to the fact that you're emotionally strong and don't break down easily. Remember that the shadow isn't just made up of "bad" things. It can include qualities like creativity, independence, and vulnerability—good qualities that may have been shamed when you were younger. Jung called the shadow "the seat of creativity," referring to the fact that it contains your potential and isn't limited to self-identified qualities (Alexander 2012).

PERSONAL VS. COLLECTIVE SHADOWS

We talked about the collective unconscious, but remember that the archetypes are all a part of this. This means that there's a collective shadow as well as your own personal shadow. Your personal shadow encompasses your individual experiences, feelings, desires, memories, and traits; the collective shadow includes all the traits that society as a whole pushes down—things like gender roles, race, and power, or things that communities or cultures deem to be unacceptable or taboo. I find it helpful to think of the shadow vertically, with the personal at the top and the collective underneath it. They're not separate; they operate on a continuum (Kamal 2024).

Two classic trends in current culture illustrate the collective shadow very well. Imagine, on the one hand, a woman who hides her ambition, and on the other, a man who hides his emotional sensitivity. This happens because of cultural pressure and social conditioning that is experienced not just by that one woman and that one man but by all of us collectively. The upshot of this is that you're carrying your own suppressed parts, as well as some that you've inherited from society as a whole.

Take a moment to consider how the collective shadow may have influenced how you see yourself. Have you ever told yourself that you can't do something because of your gender, for example? An even more uncomfortable thought experiment is to ask yourself if you've ever judged someone else, albeit silently, because of what culture has taught you is appropriate or inappropriate. Perhaps you were shocked to find that the person you hired to fix a piece of furniture was a woman, or you found it distasteful to see a grown man break down in tears. It's not easy to look at these judgments, and you might even be inclined to pretend to yourself that you've never made them, but it's okay. It's not your fault; this is the collective shadow at work, and in order to change, you must first acknowledge what's happening.

SHADOW OR EGO?

Remember that the ego is conscious. Jung understood the ego to be the center of consciousness and personal identity. Because it's conscious, it's able to bridge the gap between your inner world and the outer one, and it's informed by memories, thoughts, and feelings that have not been repressed. It's an expression of self, but it's not representative of the whole thing (The Jungian Shadow 2015).

In Jungian thought, the personal unconscious is made up of different units known as "complexes." These are groups of thoughts, feelings, and memories related to different emotional themes (Johnson 2023). They're determined by our experiences and the way we react to them. You've heard, I'm sure, of the Freudian idea of the Oedipus complex, the theory that young boys compete with their fathers for their mothers' affection and attention, while girls compete with their mothers for their fathers' (Cherry 2024c). This is just one of many complexes, though. If you've ever caught yourself saying something that felt out of character and thought, "I have no idea what just came over me," this is probably a complex at work. Jung believed that the ego (on its own) is inclined to make inappropriate decisions, and that if we can bring aspects of the shadow in to balance it, we will be able to evolve. The challenge is that complexes can surface without the ego being capable of reflecting on them, and this can cause difficulties (The Jungian Shadow 2015).

When you were born, you came into the world with a physical and mental blueprint for life—certain behaviors that have evolved as humans have adapted to their environment. Jung believed that the potential of the whole personality is present from birth, and the environment merely feeds and develops what's already there (The Jungian Shadow 2015). The ego is the part of your psyche that helps you survive according to these innate instincts and be accepted by others. It shields you from anything it thinks might harm you, an idea you may have been introduced to if you've ever done any inner child work. Your inner child is a young element of your psyche that influences your thoughts and reactions as an adult (Childs 2023). Your ego is predisposed to think your inner child will harm you, and it will try to protect you from it. Dr. Nicole Lepera explores this idea in her work and advocates for the value of becoming aware of the needs of the inner child so that we can "reparent" them, which means permitting the ego to let them in (Lepera 2021).

Your ego has developed strategies to protect itself from unwanted thoughts, feelings, and traits by pushing them into the shadow, at the same time, drawing in the characteristics it deems to be good. Much of this happens in childhood through social conditioning, as we discussed earlier. This leaves us with the task, in adulthood, of integrating the contents of the shadow with the ego and modifying it so that it aligns with our values and sense of self. Your ego, though, is like an overprotective parent, and it won't allow those shadow aspects back in without a fight. It likes to be in control, and it would like you to think that you already know yourself fully, so it has developed thought patterns and behaviors that support this belief (Deaver 2020).

Shadow work is not about getting rid of the ego; it's about helping it to loosen its grip and convincing it that those traits that have been relegated to the shadow deserve to be included in the conscious self. When we do this, we're able to expand our consciousness and let go of the energy that we've been using to suppress the shadow. The result? A renewed sense of hope, self-acceptance, and the feeling that you're finally living an authentic life (Serebrennikova n.d.).

SHADOW MYTHS—WRECKED!

How long has it taken you to finally embrace the concept of shadow work? Chances are, if you've thought about exploring it in the past, you've run into at least one myth that has put you off. Perhaps you've read something that claims that it's dangerous or even demonic. Maybe you've heard that it's only about emotional pain or getting rid of your negative traits.

Perhaps you even thought you didn't have a shadow. Let's shatter all these myths before we *really* get to work. I want you to believe in the process, and these myths won't do you any favors in that regard.

Myth #1: Shadow work is dangerous

I've heard this one a lot. Many people think that because shadow work is about exploring the "dark" aspects of the self, it's dangerous. But as you know now, the shadow is not made up only of "bad" things—it's about understanding the parts of our psyche that we've hidden away from ourselves. It isn't about giving in to harmful impulses or engaging in dangerous behaviors. In fact, we're far more likely to avoid these things and make healthy decisions when we truly know ourselves (Shadow Work Mythbusting n.d.).

Myth #2: Shadow work is for people with deep emotional pain or trauma

It's certainly true that people who have endured trauma can benefit from shadow work, but they're not the only ones. Every single person has a shadow self, and when we seek to understand it, we have a better understanding of and relationship with ourselves (Shadow Work Mythbusting n.d.).

Myth #3: Shadow work is for eliminating negative traits

I've worked with many people who thought that shadow work was about getting rid of difficult emotions like fear or anger. In actuality, we're not trying to get rid of anything; we're working on integrating all the parts of the psyche, understanding and managing those challenging emotions constructively (Shadow Work Mythbusting n.d.).

Myth #4: Shadow work is lonely

The idea of having to go deep within yourself without support is a scary idea. I don't deny that this process will require a lot of self-reflection, but that doesn't mean you need to do it alone if you don't want to. You can combine this work with therapy, which may make it easier to handle some of the unsavory emotions that may arise along the way (Shadow Work Mythbusting n.d.). You can also talk to a friend or family member about the different things that come up for you, which may help you to clarify them and will certainly give you the support you're looking for.

Myth #5: You only need to do shadow work once

If only! This is an ongoing process, not a "one and done" task. If you think about it, it makes sense: You're continually experiencing new things, changing, and growing (hopefully!). Personally, I think this is quite exciting, and it's the only way to achieve continuous and lasting growth.

Myth #6: Shadow work is for warriors

Although shadow work is not for the faint of heart, you aren't going into battle with yourself; you just need to let your defenses down and tune in, listening to and trusting the unconscious elements of your psyche to come into your awareness. Truly, it's more about surrendering than it is about fighting (McHale n.d.).

Myth #7: Shadow work is dark or scary

A less common myth, but certainly one that I've run into, is that shadow work has demonic connotations. This has probably come from religion, which often forbids certain behaviors or feelings. You know already that the shadow is not inherently bad, but this view comes from the distinction between good and evil. We're not welcoming evil when we engage in shadow work; we're integrating the parts of the psyche that we've pushed away, which, ultimately, gives us more control over our behavior (Shaheen and Zweig 2024).

Myth #8: Shadow work is only for spiritual practices

There's definitely a connection between spirituality and shadow work, but this doesn't mean you need to be very spiritual or religious to benefit. You don't need any particular kind of belief system to engage in shadow work. All you need is the desire to understand yourself on a deeper level to facilitate growth (Shaheen and Zweig 2024).

Everyone has a shadow, and to be curious about it shows maturity and courage. If any of these myths have been plaguing you, lay them to rest now. Believing in this process is the only way to benefit from it, and these myths will only hold you back.

So now that you know what the shadow is, the next question is, "Why bother digging it up?" In the next chapter, I'll explain exactly why facing the shadow is so important and how ignoring it has consequences for your relationships, stress levels, and ability to live freely and authentically.

CHAPTER 2

STOP RUNNING—THE SHADOW'S ALREADY IN THE ROOM

Research has shown that unresolved emotional trauma is linked to higher rates of anxiety, depression, substance abuse, and chronic health problems (SAMHSA 2014). Why does this happen? Well, ignored shadows don't just stay hidden. They grow and spread, shaping our reactions, our relationships, and even our physical health. Facing the shadow is one of the most direct ways we can reduce our emotional suffering and build our resilience.

Let's put that into context. Let's say you broke up with your partner and left the city where you had lived together. You couldn't stay because it was too painful, so you left and started to build a new life for yourself in a different city. Now, you avoid that city like the plague, even turning down invitations from friends just to avoid revisiting those painful emotions. One day, there's a wedding you just can't get out of, so you force yourself to go back, but you find yourself plagued by anxiety on the way. This is the unprocessed emotion in your shadow calling for your attention. Running from it hasn't helped you at all. In fact, now you're at its whim.

In this chapter, we're going to explore this concept. Shadow work is the path to freedom, clarity, and emotional strength. It's not about trying to fix something that's broken in you (because nothing is); it's about reclaiming the parts that you've been running away from.

FACING THE SHADOW

Facing the shadow changes everything, yet it's not something many of us feel all that enthusiastic about doing. Indeed, many people are scared that facing their emotional baggage will only bring them pain. It puts a whole new spin on the expression, "being afraid of your own shadow," doesn't it? On the contrary, though, confronting the hidden parts of our psyche actually helps us to develop our emotional strength, trust ourselves more, and build healthier relationships. Let's break this down.

Emotional trauma is created when an event or series of experiences is too overwhelming for the ego to assimilate, and it can leave you with memories and emotions that are repressed or dissociated. Oftentimes, they're absorbed into your shadow, leaving you feeling fragmented and alienated from your authentic self. You might be thinking at this point, "But nothing that bad has ever happened to me." I've heard this many times. But any event that overwhelms you or makes you feel isolated can traumatize you, even if there isn't a threat to your safety or security.

For some people, trauma is created by an objectively horrific event like abuse, an accident, or an attack, but for many others, it's caused by a subjective emotional experience (Robinson et al. 2025). It could be literally anything. What I want you to do here is not look for evidence of trauma in your memory, but to think about the symptoms that signal that it's there. Of course, there's the added challenge that we don't all react to trauma in exactly the same way. That would be far too easy! Nevertheless, there are some signs that are worth paying attention to (Robinson et al. 2025):

- Fear and anxiety
- Shame, guilt, or self-blame
- Mood swings, anger, or irritability
- Denial, disbelief, confusion, or shock
- Difficulty concentrating
- Drawing away from other people
- Feelings of hopelessness or sadness
- Feeling numb or disconnected from yourself and others
- Difficulty sleeping and/or nightmares
- Fatigue
- A racing heart
- Aches, pains, and muscle tension
- Feeling jumpy or on edge

Feel any of these symptoms for any length of time, and it's going to take its toll on your mental and physical health. You might think, "It's okay to live with feeling guilty; it's not doing me any harm," but if you don't address that guilt, it's going to ultimately undermine your sense of self-worth. Or perhaps you think, "I can avoid feeling on edge all the time by just not going to the places that make me feel that way." Sure, you can. But what are you sacrificing in the process?

Trauma is often like a heavy weight that you're dragging through life. Even years after the event, you might have recurring memories or dreams about it, and it probably distorts the way you see yourself and the world. We can see this clearly in the example of someone being attacked by a dog. They had no trouble with dogs before the event, but now, they're nervous about all dogs. In fact, they'll do everything they can to not be anywhere near one. They're reluctant to go to a friend's house if they have a dog, and if they see one in a park, they feel their heart racing, even though they know, rationally, that the dog's on a leash and they're probably going to be safe. This is trauma, and it's affecting that person's perception and their experience of life.

In this example, the trauma isn't just affecting the person's mind. It's also having a physical effect. Every time they see a dog, their stress response is activated. Over time, this could elevate their blood pressure, weaken their immune system, and increase their risk of cardiovascular problems (Pietrangelo 2023). If their sleep or appetite is also disrupted, which is a common response to trauma, the physical toll is likely to be even greater.

Let's say your trauma stems from being betrayed by someone you once trusted. It makes sense that this might make you wary of other people, and this could easily affect your relationships. Without even realizing it, you might be pushing people away because you're scared of being hurt again. Additionally, many people may become withdrawn and keep to themselves to help them manage their anxiety (Robinson et al. 2025).

The only solution to all of this is to resolve the pain you've been suppressing and release that energy. The shadow must be addressed. If you're still thinking that there's "nothing to see here," it could be that you're denying your trauma. Trauma denial is a strategy for distancing yourself from the experience, and it's very often unconscious. It's a natural defense mechanism, and, to that extent, it's probably working. Therapist Megan Turner says that trauma denial can bring short-term benefits because it allows you to get on with your life and avoid the painful emotions, "but the problem is that it will ultimately create a barrier to the ability to heal from the trauma" (Lebow 2021).

If you've ever found yourself minimizing your trauma, avoiding conversations about it, or trying to rewrite the narrative in your head, there's a high chance that you're in trauma denial (Trauma Denial: What Is It and Why Does It Happen 2024). Your ego is focused on survival, and it naturally perceives your traumatic memories and intense emotions as a threat; it's creating barriers to protect you. It's doing a good job: You probably feel some sense of control; you've been able to get on with your life or hang on in a difficult situation until you could remove yourself (Lebow 2021). The trouble is, by denying your experience, you're dishonoring yourself by adding to the unhealed wounding that already exists.

This is where shadow work comes in. We've talked about the shadow, but we haven't yet addressed what "shadow work" is. Let's fix that now. Shadow work is a process in which you explore what's behind your thoughts, feelings, and behaviors—especially the ones that make you feel uncomfortable or out of control (Wiginton 2024). Let's move away from trauma and its symptoms for a moment. Let's say you keep snapping at your friend, and you're not sure why it's happening. That's the kind of thing that shadow work can help you figure out.

I won't claim that it's going to be rainbows and unicorns. It's going to be much tougher than that—but it's going to be much more rewarding too. And anyone who claims that shadow work is fun or easy is lying to you—so run as fast as you can in the opposite direction and hang on to your wallet! You're not in this for the glitter and bubble gum. You're in it for learning the root causes behind your emotional responses and behaviors and healing from the trauma you may not even realize you're carrying. You're in it for discovering your untapped potential, developing healthy coping strategies, improving your relationship with yourself and others, and learning how to set healthy boundaries (Wiginton 2024). You're in it for silencing that self-deprecating voice in your head and discovering that the antidote is within the poison. In my opinion, that's far better than glitter and bubble gum, and it's worth feeling a little uncomfortable for a while.

THE COST OF AVOIDING YOUR SHADOW

Your shadow doesn't disappear just because you try to ignore it. In fact, you'll probably find that it fights back harder. An ignored shadow could lead to low self-esteem and self-loathing, a tendency to deceive yourself and/or others, and difficulty in forming healthy relationships. It can also lead to depression and anxiety, self-sabotage, and an inflated ego (Garoutte-Mohammed 2024).

Suppressed emotions have a tendency to leak out in weird ways and at inconvenient times. Sadness, for example, might manifest as burnout, which you could attribute to any number of things without realizing that the true cause is the sadness you're refusing to acknowledge in yourself. You might also find yourself feeling numb or empty on a regular basis without being able to pinpoint the cause (Raypole 2024). To avoid feeling your suppressed sadness, your subconscious may steer you to avoid talking about your feelings or putting yourself in situations where they might be triggered—and if they *are* triggered, you might find yourself engaging in behaviors you'd rather not display.

Passive aggressiveness is one of these. Often when there's anger hidden beneath the surface, it bubbles up as passive-aggressive behavior—behavior that's seemingly neutral but which displays unconscious aggression nonetheless (Cherry 2025). If you've ever answered, "I'm fine," when, really, you weren't, or you've resisted someone asking you to do something by procrastinating heavily, you've been showing passive aggression, probably without even realizing it.

Of course, it isn't just sadness and anger that could be hiding inside your shadow. Fear is a common one, too. You might walk away from a great job opportunity, officially because you want to spend more time with your family, when really, the reason is that you're subconsciously afraid of failing, and you're engineering a way to keep yourself away from the risk.

It's common for people who ignore their shadow to project onto other people, too. By this, I mean that they see things in other people that they may not even recognize within themselves. Maybe you find yourself drawn to point out flaws in other people that are actually insecurities of your own. If you catch yourself calling someone stupid, it could be that it's your own insecurity about your intelligence speaking. If you whisper to a friend that someone else's outfit looks terrible, you might really be reassuring yourself that you wouldn't be caught looking that way. Don't feel bad if you recognize any of these behaviors as being things you've done. There's no shame here. There's a reason it happens, and this is what we're here to address. Our insecurity takes over, and we're seeking reassurance that we would never do the thing we're judging someone else for (Othon 2023). It's important to note that not all observations about others are projections, though; sometimes, there's a lot to be said for calling a spade a spade.

Being quick to anger with people who can't fight back is common, too. Have you ever yelled at a customer service agent on the phone when they've done nothing personally to anger you? Your shadow may have been exerting its power over that person to compensate for your feeling of helplessness. Falling prey to victim mentality is another one. A lot of people will go to great lengths to portray themselves as the wronged party rather than admit that what they did was wrong, and very often, they can't even admit that to themselves (Othon 2023).

Our shadows may also give us prejudices and biases we're barely aware of—ones that we don't want to acknowledge. It's human nature to form assumptions about people based on their appearance, but it's possible to take this too far and slip into toxic prejudice. We'd never want to think we were prejudiced against a particular group of people, so it's often easier to pretend that we're not rather than do the work it would take to rewrite our unconscious biases (Othon 2023). We might, however, cut in front of someone in line at the grocery store, believing ourselves, on some unconscious level, to be more worthy of being served first, telling ourselves that we're in a rush for something important, perhaps, and they're unlikely to have the same demands on their time. That's our unconscious bias taking over.

The unaddressed shadow can also explain the messiah complex. When people believe they do nothing wrong and all their actions are designed to help all the people they believe need saving in some way, this is a form of "spiritual bypassing." This is when we hide behind our spiritual beliefs to avoid handling our own uncomfortable emotions or wounds (Toniolo 2020).

An ignored shadow will make lots of noise all on its own. Pretending the shadow doesn't exist and letting it just sit there unhealed is a guarantee that it will rear its head in ugly ways. Your shadow isn't going anywhere, and it's going to keep controlling your life in one way or another until you finally make the conscious choice to heal and integrate it once and for all.

SHADOW WORK FOR INNER PEACE

You might think that inner peace would mean avoiding your most difficult emotions. After all, how can you feel peace if you're angry or sad? Unfortunately, though, it's not that simple. Learning to handle challenging emotions compassionately is necessary, but first, you must become aware of them.

Healing trauma begins with self-awareness—a conscious understanding of your character, thoughts, feelings, desires, and beliefs (Li et al. 2021). These have been developing since infancy into a complex system inside you (Addressing the Self: The Importance of Self-Awareness for Healing n.d.). We don't become self-aware overnight, and we need to show ourselves compassion as we develop it. We must accept where we are right now in order to evolve. Everyone starts somewhere and at some time, and there's no judgment around where or when you begin. You've begun, that's the important part, and most people won't even get to that point. Showing ourselves love and acceptance is the foundation upon which we can learn and grow (Williams n.d.).

Self-compassion has actually been shown to reduce the symptoms of PTSD and facilitate post-traumatic healing. Researchers have found that it helps to reframe our experience of suffering as part of a shared human experience, and this can help us to see the traumatic event in a new light (Adonis et al. 2025). As I mentioned earlier, we're all having both a personal and a collective human experience, equating to both a personal and a collective shadow. By changing perspective from the microcosm to the macrocosm, we can develop a broader understanding of our experiences, relieving us of some of the personal pain.

Finding inner peace requires integrating the shadow and letting go of long-held limiting beliefs (Valverde n.d.). Shadow work doesn't eliminate all of our triggers immediately, but over time, those triggers can soften their grip and help us to accept the parts of ourselves we've been hiding from and integrate them into our identity (Tap Into Your Dark Side with Shadow Work 2023). Finding inner peace does not require you to do anything perfectly, though. The goal is to be real, integrated, and whole, and that's what shadow work can bring us.

FROM AWARENESS TO STRENGTH

I've talked several times about the importance of integrating your shadow into your conscious self, but what does it really mean? Shadow integration is about recognizing, accepting, and learning from your suppressed and repressed experiences and emotions by bringing them to light and healing them instead of fighting them. By bringing these disowned parts of yourself back into your conscious awareness and resolving those tensions, you become whole instead of fragmented (Jefferey 2025a).

Imagine a situation when you feel your anger rising because someone is lying to you. You might think, "I wouldn't do that." But what does your shadow have to say about this? Perhaps this aspect is lurking in your shadow, and when you confront it, you find that, actually, you lie too—even to yourself. Once you've recognized and accepted this part of yourself, your anger isn't going to be so quick to jump out of its box when someone else does it. You're going to have to go through many confrontations like this to integrate your shadow. It won't happen overnight, and you'll need to practice patience.

Anger, surprisingly, is a helpful emotion. It can aid us in setting healthy boundaries and reinforcing them. The thing is, we must work with it to get this benefit. If it's repressed, we'll find it rearing its head in all sorts of unhelpful ways, but if we use it well, it can be a tool for protecting the things we value and helping others when they're being mistreated. Integrated anger redirected outward provides the emotional energy we need to motivate boundary setting. When anger is unexpressed, unprocessed, and repressed, we have a hard time setting boundaries or responding to injustices in a resilient way (McLaren n.d.).

Aggression gives us another helpful example. It's a characteristic many of us have in our shadow, and we're in dire need of integrating it. The thing about aggression is that we associate it with violence—but when we do this, we're only looking at one side of the issue. There's a healthy form of aggression too, one that fuels positive transformation. It strengthens us when we're facing fear, oppression, and disrespect and gives us the drive to honor ourselves and reclaim our power and sovereignty. The energy behind aggression is a catalyst for change, enabling us to transmute that energy into positive action.

Most of us weren't taught this, though. We learned from a young age that acting out would result in negative consequences, so we pushed those feelings down to reduce conflict and do what was expected of us. Ironically, though, all this means is that our aggression lurks in the shadow and makes us susceptible to situationally inappropriate and exaggerated bouts of rage and anger. We can't use this energy to fuel our sense of purpose and wholeness, though, while it's confined to the shadow (How to Integrate Your Shadow—The Dark Side Is Unrealized Potential 2020). This energy must be set free— expressed, acknowledged, and understood—to then transform, heal, and be integrated to serve higher aims. Integrated aggression leads to courage, confidence, and purposeful action—and who wouldn't want that?

Getting to know your shadow and integrating it into your consciousness will require many ego deaths and rebirths until you ultimately become your authentic self. You'll need to confront your ego to let the shadow in and acknowledge the shadow aspects prior to healing and integration. You've been building your ego for many years, and dismantling it is going to take conscious and methodical moves—because there will be inevitable resistance along the way. "No," you might say to yourself. "That's not me. I'm not like that." This is your ego standing its ground and keeping your old identity safe and in familiar places, but it's not as unbreakable as it may seem (Jeffery 2025a).

You may encounter fear, discomfort, and reluctance when you start to face the traits hidden in your shadow. You might want to run from this, but don't! Make a conscious effort to tell yourself that there is healing on the other side, and allow yourself to explore why you're feeling this resistance. Your mind is trying to protect you from the uncomfortable feelings that arise when you confront the difficult experiences, emotions, and insecurities buried within you (The Ultimate Guide to Shadow Work Journaling 2025). Your resistance is telling you something. Perhaps it's highlighting your fear of being judged, or maybe it's alerting you to painful memories. The resistance itself can give you a deeper understanding of who you are if you're willing to recognize and honor it by listening to what it has to say.

Everyone has different levels of resistance when it comes to shadow work. This process is not for the faint of heart but for those willing to be brutally honest with themselves and move forward with their eyes wide open. There are five common aspects that determine the level of resistance: sincerity, curiosity, effort, energy, and the center. Let me explain. For shadow work to be successful, the most important thing is that you're sincere—that you genuinely want to know yourself on a deeper level and integrate every aspect of who you are. The trickster archetype can get in the way here, making you *think* you want to do this when really, you're not so committed. This will stand in your way. The second factor, curiosity, follows on from this. Are you truly curious to know who you are, regardless of whether you like all of it? If you are, you have a strong weapon against your internal resistance (Jeffery 2025a).

Shadow work takes effort, and you must be dedicated to addressing your shadow even when it's inconvenient. As I mentioned before, shadow work is ongoing, not a "one and done" deal. When you're not willing to put in this effort, you're creating a layer of resistance. The same is true if you're unable to give it enough energy. If your attention is drawn to other places, this work will be arduous if it even happens at all. Consciously making the time and holding the mental space for this work are non-negotiables. Lastly, we need to be centered, observing ourselves and accepting each part without reaction or judgment. Otherwise, we're resisting the process, and our progress will be limited (Jeffery 2025a).

Not only are there factors determining our levels of resistance, but there's a way to move through it. First, we must recognize and honor the resistance. Oftentimes, there's trauma behind it, and you should be kind to yourself while accepting its presence. Allow it to be seen fully, feeling all the emotions caught inside it. Resistance is an opportunity for transmutation. Why are you resisting at this moment? Are there feelings of sadness or shame beneath the surface? It won't be comfortable, but to release these feelings completely, you must first feel them with all of your being (Lohret, n.d.). It's easy to think that the very nature of feelings is that we feel them when they're present, but in truth, most of us are naturally inclined to do everything we can *not* to feel uncomfortable emotions. Shadow work asks that we change this pattern.

Remember, too, that taking on shadow work is a choice. No one is forcing you to do it; you don't *have* to do it, and most people don't. You're doing it because you made a conscious decision. Remind yourself of this when you become aware of your resistance. Very often, your resistance tries to do the opposite of what you're working toward accomplishing. Let's say you're committed to being healthier, and you've signed up for a gym membership and a healthy eating program. Your resistance may find ways for you not to get to the health food store or the gym. It's essentially sabotaging you. Recognize the self-sabotage so you can work through the resistance (Lohret n.d.).

Whew! That's some pretty intense stuff, but don't let it discourage you. Shadow integration may make us uncomfortable at times, but it's not a dramatic process. It happens quietly and gradually with every small choice and reflection we make day by day. You are a limitless being with infinite potential—not only capable of the change you seek but infinitely more. You're stronger than you realize, and you're definitely strong enough to overcome the resistance and dissonance between the shadow and the ego.

So now you know why shadow work matters, and this leads us to a new question: "Where's the shadow hiding?" That's what we'll look at now. You're going to learn how to spot shadow patterns in your life—even the sneaky ones that really want you to overlook them!

CHAPTER 3

SPOTTING YOUR INNER SABOTEUR

Studies show that 95% of cognitive activity happens in the subconscious mind (Zaltman 2003). This means that most of your decisions, emotional reactions, and behaviors are influenced by emotions and beliefs you may not even be fully aware of. The shadow is hidden in the subconscious mind; it contains your programming and runs programs of beliefs you hold in the background every day, shaping your decisions and behavior (Molitor 2019). You may not know (yet!) what's hidden in your shadow, but you see evidence of it all the time. So just how are we going to solve this conundrum? How will you find the shadow you meet every day without recognizing it? We'll start by finding a mirror.

THE MIRROR GAME

You can spot your shadow in other people. Not because it likes to hang out with your friends when you're not paying attention, but because other people are like mirrors, reflecting back the qualities hidden in ourselves. What annoys or angers you the most in other people is often (but not always) a reflection of something you're not acknowledging about yourself. As Jung himself said, "Everything that irritates us about others can lead us to an understanding of ourselves" (Oppong 2023). It's a pathway to self-awareness.

Let's say you have a friend who's always late. You know this, expect it even, yet it irritates you every time. This may be because punctuality is an important value to you and it's a standard you uphold for yourself, sometimes at great cost. When your friend is late, it feels as though they don't value your time. What about if you're annoyed by someone who's very outspoken? Could it be that you don't feel comfortable expressing your own views, and you have subconscious resentment toward them for being able to do this when you can't? Or could it be because you don't feel so sure about your own beliefs, and their certainty amplifies your feelings of insecurity?

Poet and novelist Hermann Hesse, who was drawn to Jungian ideas, said, "If you hate a person, you hate something in him that is part of yourself. What isn't part of ourselves doesn't disturb us" (Woolfe 2016). In other words, in our example, you wouldn't be upset by your acquaintance being outspoken if this quality didn't reflect something you didn't like in yourself. We can learn more about ourselves by paying attention to how we react to other people and exploring why we react that way. The next time your friend is late and you feel your irritation bubbling, you can take a step back and ask yourself, "Why am I bothered by this?" Once we achieve self-awareness, we're in a position to change our reaction (Oppong 2023).

One thing we have to remember here, however, is that sometimes people behave badly, and our judgment is justified. As I said, not everything is projection. That judgment is not necessarily the same thing as having an emotional reaction to a behavior in someone else that reflects something inside ourselves (Woolfe 2016). Reactions, especially those that are disproportionate to the situation, stem from the subconscious shadow; judgments, on the other hand, stem from the ego, where conscious cultural and personal beliefs are held. To make things even more confusing, some judgments are masked projections: those stemming from moral superiority or rigid thinking. Other judgments are actually accurate discernment (Wilber 2000). Our job is to refine our ability to tell the difference between them all (Tolle 2010).

In the last chapter, we talked about projections and resistances. These two things are often bound up together. Projection, as we discussed, is when we attribute qualities hidden in ourselves onto other people. If we're reacting to or judging (in certain instances) someone for being rude, we may very well be doing this as a defense mechanism to help us avoid confronting rudeness in ourselves. Can you see how the projection and the resistance are happening in the same behavior here? This is a powerful tool when we can recognize it: We can find out where our reactions and certain judgments are coming from and deliberately choose not to resist the shadow aspects behind them (Woolfe 2016).

What's important to remember here is that there's a reason we're wired to project onto others. It's a protective strategy that externalizes our difficult emotions, thereby meaning that we don't have to consciously acknowledge them. This is our ego at work. It's trying to protect itself from feeling pain (Wong 2023). This doesn't mean we should give in to it, though. It simply means we have to treat ourselves (and therefore our egos) with compassion as we move through this process and develop our self-awareness.

Addressing a Projection

The next time you feel a strong emotional reaction to someone else's behavior, try working through this process (Rankin n.d.):

1. **Recognize that you're projecting.** Ask yourself, "What emotions am I feeling?," and "What thoughts am I having?" You're going to have to dig deep. What are you *really* feeling? It might not be what's at the surface. What's your reaction really about? You may not be able to get to this immediately. You might need to talk it out with a friend or explore it in a journal; you might need to delve into a similar reaction multiple times. The important thing is, you're paying attention and you're asking the right questions.
2. **Pay attention to the different parts of yourself.** Remember that when we project onto others, we're really trying to avoid our own difficult emotions, and for healing to happen, we must bring them into the light so that we can address them. It's going to involve asking yourself some tough questions. For example, you might ask yourself, "Is there a chance that I'm blaming my partner for hating men when the truth is, I have a part that's misogynistic?" Is there anything you're afraid to see or acknowledge inside yourself? What parts of you are being activated? I want you to ask yourself questions and look for evidence in the different parts of yourself, but I want you to do so without judgment. Treat yourself with compassion and curiosity, and allow yourself to feel any emotion that comes up along the way.
3. **Hold yourself accountable.** If you're in a cycle of projection, the best way to break it is to own it when you notice it happening rather than placing blame on

the other person. This isn't easy (after all, it's happening subconsciously!), but steps 1 and 2 should help you to recognize it. Bonus points if you can own up to the other person as well as to yourself!
4. **Accept your emotions.** There's huge power in owning your emotional experience, and once you do this, you'll be able to reflect on the emotion and heal the wounds beneath the surface. Why is it rising up in you? What underlying beliefs or past experiences are fueling it? Once you accept these emotions as yours, you can respond (not react) to the other person in a more rational way, and you're more likely to hear and see what they're really saying and doing rather than what you're projecting onto them.

THE FEELINGS THAT REVEAL YOUR SHADOW

There could be many things hidden in your shadow, but there are some specific emotions that are often clear signals. These are called "shadow emotions" (Nicogossian 2021). The advantage of seeing them as shadow emotions rather than negative emotions is that we create a block for ourselves when we label our emotions as negative. No wonder we want to suppress them if they're negative! Let's take anger as an example. In the last chapter, we saw that anger is a helpful emotion if it's recognized, expressed, processed, integrated, and used appropriately. It's one of the emotions commonly hidden in the shadow because we've been conditioned to think that it's negative, and this prevents us from using it constructively. But if we see anger as a *shadow* emotion rather than a *negative* one, inviting it into our conscious awareness doesn't seem so bad.

There are five categories of shadow emotion: anger, sadness, anxiety/fear, disgust, and embarrassment/shame (Nicogossian

2021). They're not always comfortable emotions to feel, but that doesn't mean they're bad, and it doesn't mean they don't have utility. We have to accept and bring them into our conscious awareness in order to heal old wounds, change destructive behaviors, and understand our full experience. Really, all these emotions are asking of us is that we recognize them and take care of them—if we don't, they're just going to get louder and show up when we're not prepared to deal with them (Nicogossian 2021).

Our emotional experience holds a light up to the things we need to pay attention to. We're quite happy to pay attention to the emotions we've labeled positive—ones like joy and happiness—but what about the information held in the emotions we don't enjoy so much? They have just as much, if not more, to tell us. No emotion is inherently good, and no emotion is inherently bad. They're just data points, and if we want to understand ourselves and our needs, we need to pay attention to them—all of them (Fairbank 2021).

This all starts with identifying your shadow emotions. You can do this by labeling each emotional experience you have. Describe how you're feeling in detail. Don't stop at "I'm feeling sad." What is that sadness like? Does it include feelings of loneliness, exhaustion, or hopelessness, for example? The more specific you can get, the more self-awareness you'll develop. Pay attention to the thoughts that come up with those emotions as well. Are you being critical about yourself, others, or a situation? Is your judgment a masked projection or an accurate assessment? Are your thoughts tied to a past experience or worries about the future? Do your best not to judge yourself as you do this. This may be difficult, so be aware of your conditioning and how you've been taught to view the emotion. Were you ever told it was wrong or a sign of weakness to show this emotion? Has it been met with a negative reaction in the past?

Awareness of this programming is needed to embrace these shadow emotions. Remember, the emotion you're exploring doesn't define you; all you have to do is accept it with compassion (Nicogossian 2021).

THE 3-STEP SHADOW SKILL DRILL

Let's reduce all of this down into a simple exercise. It isn't so simple, of course. As you've seen, it's necessary to acknowledge and embrace some unsavory emotions and then ask yourself lots of tough questions while being brutally honest yet compassionate with yourself. But we can refine the process to make it a 3-step method that you can turn to easily. I'd recommend saving it in your phone or writing it on a sticky note so that you can revisit it whenever you like:

1. Notice your emotional reaction.
2. Ask yourself, "Have I felt this before? What does it remind me of?"
3. Reflect on what fear or need could be hiding beneath it.

Spotting your shadow is the beginning of this work, but we have much more to do. Now that you see the program that's been running in the background, it's time to prepare to face it with more intention and support, and for that, you're going to need to feel emotionally safe and mentally strong. In the next chapter, we'll work on building your mindset and creating a place of emotional safety so that you can go deeper.

CHAPTER 4

BEFORE THE DIG—SETTING THE GROUND FOR INNER WORK

Now that you've begun to recognize your shadow, it's time to start the real work, but engaging in emotional processing without first establishing a sense of psychological safety is a sure way to feel overwhelmed, which could cause you to walk away from the healing process (Veale et al. 2023). We don't want that, so what we're going to do now is secure your emotional safety. If you don't feel safe, you're less likely to be able to do the work properly. The truth is, shadow work isn't about being tough—it's about being prepared.

BUILDING YOUR INNER SANCTUARY

When I talk about your inner sanctuary, what I mean is a mental and emotional space where you feel grounded, safe, and calm. If you think about the literal definition of a sanctuary, it's a place where you're safe from danger. When you have this, you go about your life with a different perspective from someone who doesn't feel safe—and it's the same with emotional safety. Your inner sanctuary is reflected in your physical body when you feel peace—a drop in your shoulders, perhaps, or the feeling of calm, steady breathing (Roberts 2023). It's a symbolic place in your psyche where you can access your truth, hold your emotions and memories, and explore all the parts of yourself gently and safely (Carter n.d.). You need a peaceful inner space before you'll be ready to explore your deeper emotions, and there are several ways you can create it.

Visualizations

Neither the mind nor the body has an easy time distinguishing between reality and the imagination, and this is something we can take advantage of. To see how powerful this is, visualize yourself holding a big chunk of lemon and biting into it. Pay attention to how your body responds. See how powerful your imagination is? This is something you can use to make you feel safe and build your inner resilience and confidence, and I'm going to walk you through a couple of exercises that will help you with this.

Visualize a Safe Place (Rees n.d.):

1. Prepare your body by sitting up straight, closing your eyes, and breathing gently and rhythmically. Keep your chest open and your shoulders back, and try to smile a little.
2. Visualize a safe image in your mind. This may take a moment, and different images may drift into your mind before you settle on something.
3. Pay attention to how the safety feels in your body as you focus on the image. Can you pinpoint where it's coming from? Once you've done this, allow it to flow through the rest of you, keeping in mind the knowledge that you're safe and that this safe space will always be here for you.

4. Bring all your senses into the image you're visualizing. What can you see? What can you smell or feel on your skin? Immerse yourself in this experience.
5. Move your fingers and toes, and pay attention to how the image fades away while remembering that you can always get back to it. Open your eyes.
6. Reflect on your experience. Did you notice any changes, either in your emotions or in your body? Pay particular attention to any resistance you felt.

Safe Place Meditation (Birk n.d.):

Sit somewhere comfortable with your feet on the floor. Make sure your body feels fully supported and you're not having to tense to hold the position. Focus on your breathing, paying attention to what it's doing right now and which parts of your body move with it (this may change a little while you're focusing on it). Now make each inhalation and exhalation longer, particularly the exhalations (this will calm your parasympathetic nervous system).

Once you've found a rhythm with your breathing, tune in to what you're thinking, labeling each thing as a "thought." Turn your focus back to your breathing. Now visualize a safe place (this could be a place you have real experience of, or you could imagine it). The conditions of this place are up to you, but you should feel completely safe there. Use your senses to explore. What can you see? What can you smell? What can you hear? Are there textures to focus on? Is there a taste you can tune in to? Try to give something to each of your senses, even if you have to borrow a smell and a taste from another experience. Spend some time doing this and enjoying the sensations that come from it. This will help you to stay grounded and let your brain simulate the experience of being in a relaxed state in this safe place. Stay here for a while, keeping your breath constant and visualizing the scene.

Both of these exercises will give you an idea of a safe place you can come back to whenever you need to. This doesn't mean you can't change your image if you want to, but it will give you a starting point. Visit this place regularly so that it's clear in your mind and you can access it easily. Each time you do so, allow the details to unfold without judging your thoughts or emotions. This is a place you can come back to in order to help you regulate your emotions whenever they feel overwhelming or your thoughts are disruptive. As you see that you can do this whenever you choose, you'll begin to trust yourself more, which will build your self-awareness and make you more open to the different aspects of yourself (Rennell 2024).

Breathing Techniques

In the visualization exercises, you concentrated on your breathing to focus your mind and prepare your body to enter the safe space. We can use breathing in isolation, too, to help us find our inner sanctuary. When you breathe deeply, your body understands that it's safe to relax, and this will make it easier for you to think clearly and handle intense emotions (Grounding Strategies n.d.). We'll go through two simple techniques now.

4-7-8 Breathing

This is a form of pranayamic breathing, which is designed to regulate the breath and encourage relaxation (Fletcher 2024).

1. Sit comfortably with the tip of your tongue resting on the tissue behind your top front teeth.
2. Exhale to empty your lungs.
3. Breathe in through your nose for four seconds.

4. Hold your breath for seven seconds.
5. Exhale through your mouth for eight seconds, allowing yourself to make a whooshing sound as you do so.
6. Repeat the exercise four times.

Focused Breathing

This is a calming technique that can relax you when you're feeling stressed or anxious, and it's something you can use to calm yourself down immediately in any situation (Breathing Exercises for Stress 2022).

1. Sit comfortably with your feet hip-width apart and your arms resting on the arms of the chair.
2. Allow your breath to flow as far into your belly as you can without trying to force it.
3. Breathe in through your nose, and exhale through your mouth gently and consistently. If this is tricky, try counting from one to five on each inhalation and exhalation.
4. Keep this cycle going for five minutes.

Physical Rituals

Your inner sanctuary is primarily in your psyche, but it can be more powerful and easier to access if you also create a physical space that mirrors it. This may be particularly helpful in the beginning, when it may be more difficult to call on your inner sanctuary instantaneously (Carter n.d.). Choose somewhere private and quiet at home where you can be alone, and give it a calm ambience. Ideally, this space will have ample natural light because this will lift your mood and bring you a sense of tranquility (Tips for Crafting an At-Home Meditation Sanctuary 2020). You can use soft lights, plants, and soothing colors to build the ambience further, and you can make it your own by adding meaningful photos, ornaments, or artwork. This can be anything you like. It should reflect your personality and bring you a sense of comfort and joy. Your space should also be comfortable, so add large cushions or blankets—whatever will make you feel relaxed and supported—and you can help yourself to stay grounded in it by using scented candles or essential oils to engage your sense of smell (Tips for Crafting an At-Home Meditation Sanctuary 2020).

You don't want to take your phone into this space or have kids, pets, or anyone else running in every five minutes, so make sure that you have a door you can close, and leave technology outside. Within this space, you can then set up rituals that will signal to your mind that you're about to tune in to your inner world. Maybe you'll do a breathing exercise or light a candle—it's up to you, but the ritual will help you transition into your inner sanctuary (Carter n.d.).

CURIOSITY, NOT JUDGMENT

Be curious like a child: wild-eyed, wide-hearted, and full of *why*. There's nothing wrong with being curious. In fact, we need curiosity if we're going to grow, and shadow work requires it. It's our curiosity that allows us to steer ourselves away from criticism and remember that we're not trying to fix anything—we're observing what's going on inside us and understanding it. It's how we become open to new experiences, and developing this skill is much easier than you might think. You can practice this outside of your internal work by doing something like committing to learning a new thing every day. The more you learn, the more you'll want to continue the process, thereby strengthening your curiosity muscle (Campbell 2019).

When it comes to our inner work, it's curiosity that will allow us to make peace with the aspects of the shadow rather than pushing them away. Perhaps, for example, you'll ask yourself, "What's happened to you?" rather than "What's wrong with you?" instantly calling on curiosity rather than judgment. We often resort to judgment almost as a defense mechanism, and it's a reaction rather than a response. When we react like this, we build up internal tension and are more likely to shut down the process of getting to know our shadow. Curiosity helps us to remain open and encourages us to consider the broader implications (Gerbrandt n.d.). The mind, after all, can't process anything through judgment and curiosity at the same time (Myers Morgan 2020). Judgment is armed with blame and races to find a solution, whereas curiosity allows us to explore a situation, emotion, or thought pattern fully. The goal of curiosity is to understand, not to fix—remaining open, self-aware, and contemplative as you get to know your shadow aspects intimately (Myers Morgan 2020).

WHEN IT GETS UNCOMFORTABLE

There will be times throughout this process when you will feel uncomfortable, messy, or rattled. Utilizing anchoring techniques will help you stay grounded and centered when your mind gets shaken. Having grounding techniques up your sleeve will help you to reduce your anxiety and focus on the present (Cleveland Clinic 2024). This isn't to say that the anxiety will dissipate entirely, but anchoring techniques will help to alleviate some of the stress you encounter and help calm your nervous system. Here are a few techniques you can use to ground yourself when things become overwhelming (Sutton 2022):

Focus on Your Senses

We called on our senses in the visualization exercise, and you can use them in the same way to connect yourself with the present moment and pull your focus away from your discomfort. Sit comfortably, calm your breathing, and focus your attention on each inhalation and exhalation. Now ask yourself the following questions:

1. What do I see?
2. What do I hear?
3. What do I smell?
4. What do I taste?
5. What can I feel?

Hold an Object

An object is something that's outside yourself, and using your senses to experience it fully is a powerful way to ground yourself. Some people keep a smooth stone or a piece of textured fabric with them for this purpose, but any object that pleases you to touch and fits in your hand will work. Hold the object, paying attention to how it feels and looks. Reflect on the colors and details, the texture on your skin, and how heavy or light it is. Spend some time focusing on your object to anchor you back into the present moment.

Use a Chair

Sometimes, all it takes to feel grounded is to sit, focus, and visualize. Bring your awareness to the points of your body where you're making contact with the seat and the weight of your body against it. Pay attention to the chair's texture, whether it's wooden, plastic, or fabric. Push your feet into the ground, imagining the tangles in your mind draining from your head, through your body, out the soles of your feet, and into the ground. Visualize this jumbled energy as darkness, focusing on the lightness in each body part as these tangles move through and exit.

Question Yourself

When we're feeling overwhelmed or anxious, we can become detached. We can use questions to bring us back to ourselves. You may want to do this in your head, but you might find it easier to engage if you write your answers down. Ask yourself the following questions:

1. Where am I?
2. What is the date and day of the week?
3. What season is it?
4. What's my age?
5. Where do I live?
6. Who do I live with?

Prepare a Positive Statement

All of the exercises we've discussed take place in the moment, but you can also prepare yourself in advance and have a positive statement to pull out as soon as you begin to feel overwhelmed. You might, for example, say something like, "My name is _____. I am strong and resilient. This, too, shall pass, and I will have a deeper sense of wholeness on the other side. This process will soon become easier and more comfortable. I return to *now* with calm centeredness."

BECOMING A GENTLE WARRIOR

I told you earlier that shadow work isn't about going to war, so you might wonder why I'm bringing up a warrior metaphor at this point. You're going to become a *gentle* warrior, someone who's kind to themselves in the face of discomfort. You're not going to push through the pain. You're going to feel it, having compassion for yourself (remember how important this is to healing), while gently letting these situations, emotions, and thought patterns move through you as you witness them as a conscious observer instead of as an active participant.

Higher levels of self-compassion correlate with higher levels of resilience (Roberts n.d.). Although it's something many of us may find difficult, it's no different from having compassion for a friend. Let's think about the process involved for a moment. In order to show your friend compassion, you must first notice that they're having a challenging time in some way. Know that imperfection and hardship are part of the human experience, something we can all relate to. Through these commonalities and understandings, we find compassion, not just for others, but also for ourselves (Neff n.d.).

But how exactly do you do this? First and foremost, you need to be kind to yourself, which means giving yourself validation and speaking to yourself kindly—no matter how much pain or insecurity you're feeling. It will help you to remember that challenges are inevitable and no one is perfect—yourself included. Everyone has challenges; everyone makes mistakes. Understanding this will reduce the intensity of your emotions and make it easier for you to show yourself compassion. Mindfulness will help you too. You'll learn more about this in the next chapter, but the basic idea is that you observe all of your feelings and thoughts and accept them for what they are without passing judgment on them or denying them. It's easier to be kind to yourself if you're mindful of your experience, even when that experience is internal (Roberts n.d.).

Still about as clear as mud? Here are some simple ways to build your ability to show yourself compassion (Roberts n.d.):

- Give yourself a 10-second hug, or hug someone you love (it could also be a pet or a stuffed animal). This will cause your brain to release oxytocin, the hormone that makes you feel loved and connected.
- Reframe your critical thoughts as loving comments if you make a mistake.
- Say no to other people when you need to look after yourself.
- Spend time with people who make you feel good.
- Write a list of all the things you've achieved today rather than focusing on what you didn't get done.

Here are some self-compassion questions you can ask yourself to help you further (Tartakovsky 2014):

- How would I like to feel, and what can I do to generate this feeling?
- What can I do for myself when I feel sad or stressed out?
- What do I need right now?
- Are there any stories I'm telling myself that aren't helping me, and if so, how can I reframe them?
- Is there an emotion I'm finding hard to deal with?
- What new habit could I build to make me feel more calm?
- What would I say to someone else who was struggling with this?
- What are my best qualities?

If you're more of a write-it-out person, you could also try journaling your way to self-compassion. Write about times you've failed and what you learned from them. Write about the things that make you feel anxious or frightened, and explore why you feel this way about them. You can even list ways that you might show yourself more compassion or qualities you're proud of in yourself (15 Journal Prompts for Self-Compassion 2021).

SETTING INTENTIONS

Intentions are simply phrases that encapsulate what you hope to achieve from the experience, and they differ from goals in that they don't have time constraints or limitations; they're open, and they encourage *you* to be open to whatever comes up (Gooden n.d.). Setting an intention is a way to make sure your thoughts, actions, and energy are all directed toward the outcome you want to achieve.

Now, then, is the time to set an intention for your shadow work. Be clear about what you want to achieve, and focus your energy on the positive. Keep it simple, and repeat it to yourself frequently to make sure it's always clear in your mind so you can make conscious choices and align your actions with it. You'll need to be patient with yourself and persistent in your commitment to the work, but you should also be open to adjusting your intentions as you need to. To do this, ask yourself questions about the person you want to be, how you want to live, and how you want to relate to other people (The Power of Setting Intentions & How to Set Mindful Ones 2024). You might ask yourself what you want to understand about yourself or which patterns you'd like to break free from. Your intention will give you clarity about what you want to get out of this process and where you'll need to direct your energy. Remember, though, that this isn't a goal. It's more about directing yourself toward the growth you want to achieve and trusting that this is within your power (Irven n.d.).

All of this preparation work will give you the emotional footing you need to start exploring your shadow. Nonetheless, we're not going to dive in blindly. We need to use the right tools to uncover and connect with the aspects of ourselves that have been hidden in the shadow, and we need to do so gently. Are you ready? Then let's step forward with intention—not before a brief thought experiment, though!

INTEGRATING THE SHADOW TO HEAL THE WORLD

The shadow is needed now more than ever. We heal the world when we heal ourselves, and hope shines brightest when it illuminates the dark.

— SASHA GRAHAM

When we integrate our shadows, we become happier and more confident, and we untether our creative energy (Biesalski 2021). This is the future that lies ahead of you, but I want you to take a moment to consider how different the world might be if everyone were to do this. There are so many ways that the shadow shows up in our waking world: jealousy, anxiety, depression, self-sabotage, procrastination, resentment, aggression, shame, guilt …. The list goes on. Working on our shadows gives us the opportunity to heal and integrate the parts of ourselves that hurt, the parts that are hidden or unseen, and this makes them far less likely to control us by showing up in these ways.

So, again, I ask you to imagine a world in which everyone did their shadow work. It wouldn't solve all the world's problems, but it would make for happier people with better emotional regulation, a wealth of creative energy, and more personal power—an empowered world with infinite potential. That's what the future looks like. I truly believe that finding balance within and returning to wholeness leads to greater balance in the world: As within (the microcosm), so without (the macrocosm). We can lift humanity into higher levels of consciousness so that collaboration can replace competition, love can replace fear, and every single one of us is living the life we're meant to be living.

The thing I love the most about my work is helping people on an individual level, but I find it deeply satisfying to know that their healing is having a positive impact on the other people in their lives too, and I can't help but think of the profound impact this would have if more people were to do it. Energy is contagious, and it's with this in mind that I'd like to ask you a favor. Would you be willing to take a few minutes to help me get this book out to more readers? There are two ways that you can do this: Firstly, you can share it (and your own experience of shadow work, of course) with your friends and family; secondly, you can leave a short review online to help other people find it.

By leaving a review of this book on Amazon, you'll make it more visible to readers who are actively seeking ways to find inner peace, heal their trauma, and reclaim their power as their most authentic self.

Reviews help to connect books with the readers they'll help, and your words will make a huge difference. My hope is to help as many people as I can, and, in some small way, contribute to a happier, more empowered, and peaceful world. The more people who find this book, the better.

Thank you so much for your support. I appreciate it more than I can tell you. Now, let's meet that shadow!

Scan the QR code here to leave your review:

CHAPTER 5
MEETING YOUR SHADOW

Carl Jung said many wise and memorable things in his lifetime, but the one that sticks with me the most is, "There is no light without shadow and no psychic wholeness without imperfection" (The Shadow—Carl Jung's Warning to the World 2021). Sit with that one for a second. I have to nearly every time I read it. Most people spend years trying to fix, polish, and perfect themselves without realizing that the parts they're pushing away hold the missing pieces they're looking for. Finding those shadow aspects we hide from ourselves, then accepting, healing, and integrating them, is how we become whole. It's not easy work, which is why we've taken all this time to prepare. Now, though, with deeper understanding and your emotional safety taken care of, we're ready to begin—and we're going to do so not by analyzing but by communicating.

TALKING TO WHAT'S HIDDEN

We're going to start with the active imagination, a reflective process identified by Jung to allow us to talk to aspects of our unconscious. As we do this, images, emotions, and symbols are brought into our conscious awareness through the imagination, revealing "subpersonalities" we may not have realized were there (Jeffery 2025b). Jung didn't see the active imagination as a technique; he saw it as a natural process we instinctively know how to perform to bring the shadow to the light. It's a tool we can use to balance elements of the unconscious mind with the conscious one and integrate all aspects of the psyche (Jeffery 2025b). Blending the two states of consciousness like this is something we usually only do when we're dreaming, but active imagination allows us to do this while we're awake, and this can help us to identify our personal archetypes (Elass 2021).

The active imagination is a bit like a mirror that uses symbols to represent our experiences, and it holds clues as to the psychological factors that drive our behaviors and thoughts. We can use it to deal with these factors in their symbolic form and get to know what's hidden in the shadow (Krüger 2024). Although Jung was also a big believer in the power of dream analysis, this is a different process. This is also a way for us to unite our conscious and unconscious minds, and it involves considering the subject and symbolism in a dream to discover its meaning and, therefore, information about the psyche. Jung used active imagination in tandem with dream analysis to glean more information because it allows the ego to consciously interact with the symbols and imagery, which the dream ego (an unconscious agent) can't do (Jeffery 2025b).

Jung also talked about the passive imagination. With this, as with dreams, the conscious ego isn't usually in control. It runs on autopilot just as our dreams do. Essentially, it's daydreaming, a process in which we're not integrating our shadow. With the active imagination, though, the conscious ego is directly involved in communicating with the unconscious mind (Jeffery 2025b). In this process, we intentionally use our imagination to talk to parts of our unconscious mind. We take images from our dreams, but instead of analyzing them, we interact with them.

There are four layers to a psychic image: feeling, thinking, intuition, and sensation. What this means is that the symbols communicated by the unconscious mind can come to us through our emotions, inner dialogue, creative activities, and physical sensations. Using the active imagination process involves the whole body, and it requires us to ask questions, challenge the things that come up for us, and make decisions about what to do with the information. We need to hold opposing truths at the same time and maintain objectivity rather than identifying wholly with any element that arises (Krüger 2024). Remember, we're dealing with our *parts*, and the goal is to unite them to create wholeness. No one part is more "us" than any other.

So, how do we do this safely? Two key Jungian thinkers can help us with this, but bear with me a moment. We'll simplify the steps as we go. We'll start with Marie-Louise von Franz, who suggested four steps to the process (Jeffery 2025b):

1. Clear the egoic mind.
2. Allow the unconscious mind to bring up an image.
3. Give this image a way to express itself.
4. Morally engage with the image and the information it reveals.

Robert A. Johnson also proposed a four-step process, but his involved a little more structure (Jeffery 2025b):

1. Invite a specific part contained inside your unconscious mind.
2. Establish an active dialogue with it.
3. Bring your values into the dialogue.

4. Use a physical ritual to make it concrete.

Don't worry; you're new to this, and it's okay if you're not ready to make sense of either method without a little more information. We'll expand on these ideas now. Our goal is to bring ourselves to a state somewhere between wakefulness and sleep, and we're going to use the following steps to achieve it (The Active Imagination Technique: Essential Steps for Creative Exploration 2019):

1. **Focus.** Your mind is probably going to be very active at first, and your first job is to calm it so that you can control your attention and focus it on your thoughts.
2. **Bring to mind an image from a dream you've had recently.** Hold this in your mind for as long as you can, bringing your attention back to it whenever you catch your mind wandering.
3. **Let your unconscious mind speak.** Your dream image is giving you a window into your unconscious mind, and you must allow it to speak to you through the image. You'll need to loosen your grip on your focus a little to allow your unconscious mind to animate the image. As this happens, you may find yourself back in the dream narrative, or you may find yourself talking to one of the characters in the dream. These may very well represent archetypes in your psyche that are trying to alert you to information that may help you in your waking life. Be aware that this may not be comfortable: After all, you're dealing with something you may have avoided dealing with in the past.
4. **Create an object.** This can be something written, drawn, or painted. The goal is to turn the unconscious image into something you can make sense of.

5. **Interpret the object.** You're going to be using only your conscious mind now, and you're going to see if you can find the message your shadow was sending through the physical representation you've just created.

Once you've been through this process a few times, you can go deeper. You might focus on a whole dream rather than a single image to explore deeper emotions, or you might use different modalities to create your object. If, for example, you were to make something out of pottery, you'd get different physical sensations from the process, and this may allow you to see the message from a different perspective (The Active Imagination Technique: Essential Steps for Creative Exploration 2019).

The goal of the active imagination process is to bring the unconscious mind into your conscious awareness and integrate the lessons it has for you. Particularly in the beginning, you may doubt whether you're doing it "right," and this is a natural reaction: Your ego doesn't like feeling as though it's not in control, and it's only human to be wary of the unknown. You can mitigate this by making sure you're relaxed and curious before you begin; if you're highly anxious and rushing to fit it in amidst a busy schedule, you're not in the right state of mind to use the active imagination process effectively (Jeffrey 2025b). It may also take you some time to get used to dealing with the symbols and imagery. Your conscious mind deals with logic and language, and it's natural that it will take a while to communicate with symbols and imagery. Try not to use logic to figure out what the images are saying; instead, be present with them. The images contain all the information you're looking for, so all you have to do is let them present themselves (Jeffrey 2025b).

Let me try to make this process a little easier for you and give you some simple tips you can use to get started.

1. **Find a quiet, private space.** The physical place you created to access your inner sanctuary would be ideal.
2. **Write down your experience as you're having it.** Some experts recommend writing down anything spoken by characters inside your active imagination in capital letters and writing your own questions and answers in lowercase (Wilson 2023). This may make it easier to see the different parts of yourself.
3. **Anchor yourself in the image, and then wait to see who or what turns up.** You might ask them questions like, "Who are you?" or "What would you like to say?" to prompt your active imagination. Be careful not to push it in a specific direction, though; see what it has to say to you without trying to influence it.
4. **Spend time with the characters who arise.** Don't try to do this from a distance; actively participate by talking to them and experiencing the interaction as though it's real. Remember that no character has authority over you, and you don't have authority over them. Your goal is to listen.
5. **Bring your values to the interaction.** The characters in your unconscious mind won't necessarily share your values, so they'll need to be balanced by your conscious mind. To give an extreme example here, if you find yourself talking to a part of you that wants to take over the world, this isn't something your moral compass will allow the character to do. Your conscious values must be present to balance this out.
6. **Turn what you've learned into something concrete.** This is where the artistic expression we discussed earlier comes in, but you could also do this by engaging in some other kind of physical ritual that will signal to your conscious mind that you're integrating the part of your psyche you've been talking to (Wilson 2023).

You're not pretending here—you're giving form to feelings that you don't yet have words for.

THE CLUES IN YOUR DREAMS

As we've already seen, your dreams offer you glimpses into your unconscious mind. We've looked at using the imagery from them to work with our active imagination, but now we're going to turn to dream analysis. Dreams, as you know, are experiences you have when you're asleep, and they often have complex narratives. They primarily happen when you're in rapid eye movement (REM) sleep while your brain activity is heightened. During this phase, your brain is processing your emotions and memories, creating dreams in the process. No one knows for certain the purpose of dreaming, but some theorists have hypothesized that they help us to process information and consolidate memories, while others suggest that they help us to regulate our emotions and make sense of those that we may not address consciously (How to Understand Dreams and What They Reveal About Your Mental Health 2024). No matter what their function, though, dreams offer us windows into our psyche where we can interpret their symbols and narratives to gain access to our shadow aspects.

There have been several schools of thought about how dreams should be interpreted over the years, and Jung, alongside Freud, had theories that have persisted to this day. Freud was among the first psychologists to come up with a theory about dreams, and he believed that they showed us our repressed desires and thoughts. Jung developed his theories at the same time as Freud, applying his focus to archetypes and the collective unconscious. He took his theory a step further than Freud and proposed that dreams go beyond reflecting our desires and experiences and are also influenced by symbols shared among cultures. In

Jungian dream analysis, the archetypes show up as characters in our dreams and tell us more about our psyche (How to Understand Dreams and What They Reveal About Your Mental Health 2024).

There's no single way to interpret a dream, and the details of each one you have are personal to you. However, there are common dream themes and interpretations we can draw from. One of these is being chased or falling. Most people have experienced a dream like this at one time or another, and they often represent insecurity or a lack of control. If you've ever had one of these dreams at a challenging or uncertain time in your life, you can probably see the logic here. It's possible that if your dream has you running away from someone (or something) chasing you, this could suggest that you're running from something in your conscious life. Dreams about being naked in a public space are also common, and they're often linked to feelings of insecurity or vulnerability. They may also be manifestations of social anxiety. Dreams about being delayed, meanwhile (such as those about missing a plane or getting stuck in traffic), often reflect a feeling of helplessness or frustration and are common when people have obstacles standing in their way (How to Understand Dreams and What They Reveal About Your Mental Health 2024).

All of these dream themes can be quite distressing, but there are common positive ones too, flying being one of my personal favorites. Dreams about flying may represent feelings of success, empowerment, or freedom, and they're often fun. We might get them when we've had a breakthrough of some kind in our conscious life, or we feel like we're in control of things. They may also, however, symbolize a wish to break free from something that's holding us back.

One of the most fascinating types of dreams is the recurring dream. It may indicate that your subconscious is trying to draw your attention to something you haven't noticed or that needs resolution. It may reflect unprocessed trauma, long-term stress, or conflicts that have been left unresolved, and it may be that your subconscious is trying to get you to address these issues (How to Understand Dreams and What They Reveal About Your Mental Health 2024). Recurring dreams often follow similar themes to the common ones we've just discussed, like falling or being chased representing feelings of anxiety or insecurity. The fact that a dream like this reoccurs may indicate that there's something you haven't been addressing, but it also gives you extra chances to now pay attention and reconcile that part of yourself. It's always worth paying attention to recurring dreams.

The majority of our dreams, however, are not as memorable. More frequent are the ones Jung termed "compensatory dreams," dreams that compensate for what we miss with our conscious experience. The thinking here is that the more we avoid the issues we need to deal with in our waking lives, the more we'll experience compensatory dreams—for example, a parent who dreams that their children hate them may be experiencing this because their unconscious mind is trying to alert them to the fact that they're avoiding something important in their parenting (Carl Jung and the Psychology of Dreams— Messages from the Unconscious 2023).

No matter the nature of our dreams, they have something to offer us, most importantly, the opportunity to get to know our shadow. There are parts in your shadow that are very precious, parts that you've pushed down there because you associate them with a painful experience, or you're worried about social judgment or disapproval. This is known as "shadow gold" or the "golden shadow" (Laisrén 2023).

For example, a man who grew up with the message that he needed to "toughen up" every time he cried, showed fear, or expressed doubt, might have built a stoic, hyper-independent persona. As an adult, he might feel disconnected (from both other people and himself), have difficulty forming deep relationships, and often feel hollow even when he's successful. Shadow work, however, might reveal his shadow gold: The emotional sensitivity he was taught to bury is actually a powerful strength. He has the rare ability to hold space for others without judgment, and his empathy makes him a trustworthy friend, partner, and leader. He can listen deeply, sense what other people feel, and build authentic connections. If he can reclaim this trait, he can lead with his heart, rather than with logic or dominance. Essentially, what he was taught to reject is the very trait that will bring him fulfillment and connection. That's the gold in his shadow.

Shadow gold represents courage, talents, creativity, and passions that our psyche has hidden from us. These shadow aspects are often where latent potential resides (Aburrow 2021). Rarely do we recognize the hidden aspects of our greatest powers in our shadows, but there's a high chance that we'll encounter them in our dreams, just as we may recognize them in other people through projection (Laisrén 2023). We may also see a layered crossover here into a dream state. For example, if you project elements of your own shadow onto another person —say, you're angry with your boss for being arrogant because of your own suppressed ambition—your dream that night may be about climbing a tower but being unable to reach the top, revealing the origin of your anger within your buried desire for success (Drymalski n.d.).

So now we have the theory. Let's move on to the practice of remembering and interpreting dreams. We'll base this on Jungian dream analysis.

One of the most helpful things you can do is write out your dream in detail. You'll need to do this as soon as you wake up because you'll quickly forget it otherwise. A lot of people keep a dream journal by their bed for this purpose, or you could use the voice notes function on your phone and transcribe it later. You should include every detail, even if it's hard to see its importance right away. That includes the setting, the narrative, the characters, and all conversations and thoughts you had inside the dream, as well as any sensory details you recall. Once you have this, you can start to make associations between different images in the dream and aspects of your waking life. For example, if you dream about a bright yellow house and it triggers a thought about your current living situation, you might associate it with stress or anxiety, which would give you clues as to what's plaguing you in your life.

You might be inclined to consult a dream dictionary at this point, but this isn't a good idea. Every image in your dream is unique to you, and what it represents depends on your own experience and perspective. This doesn't mean, however, that you can't amplify the symbols in your dream by researching them. Jung proposed that there are three kinds of meaning you might consider here: personal (i.e., relating to childhood memories or experiences from particular times in your life), cultural (i.e., symbols used to represent particular things within your culture—like the American bald eagle to represent freedom), and archetypal (i.e., universal symbols found in all cultures—like water to represent emotion) (Brandon 2022).

At this point, you can begin to connect the images from your dream to what's happening in your internal world. Although there may be recognizable figures and settings from your waking life in your dreams, they're more likely to relate to your internal experience than they are to the literal people and places you're familiar with (Calinawan 2020). Try to think of each character as a representation of some part of you, which could include aspects of your shadow, perhaps portrayed in a new light (Williams 2025). For example, if someone you don't like appears in your dream, you might consider what it is you don't like about them. These people may represent shadow aspects within yourself.

Now you're ready to interpret your dream more completely. You may feel a little lost with this at first, but since this is all coming from within you, on some level, you know the answer, so pay attention to your intuition: If it feels like it clicks, it's probably right. Bear in mind, though, that your unconscious mind is unlikely to be sending you messages about things you already know about; the message should come as a surprise, even if it feels like the right interpretation. It's also about *you*, not about the characters in the dream, so if your interpretation leads you to place blame on others, then it's probably not correct. Each character in your dream represents something within you (Calinawan 2020). Pay attention to symbols like hiding, chasing, or conflict: These are clues, and they may signify repressed feelings or inner conflict. Notice, too, any patterns and symbols that come up across multiple dreams. Recurring animals may be significant: Think about the character traits you saw in them, and consider how they could be representative of different aspects of you (Williams 2025). Here are some questions you might ask to help yourself here (Brandon 2022):

- What did you see?
- What did you hear?
- Who did you encounter?
- What happened?
- How did you feel?
- What was the feeling the dream left you with overall?

It might also help you to imagine how your dream may have continued if you hadn't woken up, particularly if you feel like it was unfinished. You'll be using your active imagination to do this, and it may amplify the messages your subconscious mind was trying to communicate to you (Williams 2025).

When you feel happy with your interpretation, make the time to do something physical to honor it. This will help you to integrate the unconscious thoughts and emotions it represents into your consciousness (Calinawan 2020). It doesn't matter what you do here—perhaps you write about it; maybe you light a candle or create a painting. The important thing is that you're performing a physical ritual that lets your unconscious mind know that you heard it.

Of course, all of this requires you to recall your dreams in the first place. Writing them down as soon as you wake up will certainly help, but efficient dream recall starts with getting a good night's sleep that allows you to move through all the sleep stages. Dreams do occur during non-REM sleep, but you're more likely to remember them when you wake from a REM phase (Brandon 2022).

Intention matters too. If you make it an intention when you go to bed to remember your dreams and focus your attention on this, you're more likely to remember them when you wake. When you do wake up, do so gently. Focus on your dreams without letting your mind jump ahead to the day's schedule.

SHADOW JOURNALING

Writing can bring your unconscious patterns to the surface, and by exploring the answers to self-discovery questions, you can use it to get to know your shadow better (Perry 2024). Journaling, generally speaking, is a beneficial practice. Research has shown that it can reduce symptoms of stress, anxiety, and depression. In a 2006 study, young adults were asked to journal or draw for 15 minutes twice a week about an event they'd found stressful. Those who journaled found that these symptoms reduced more than they did in those who drew (Chan and Horneffer 2006). This is because it works on two levels: It helps us explore our deeper feelings and make sense of our suppressed thoughts by putting them into words. It requires us to be open about our emotions rather than keeping them buried, and it encourages us to organize our experiences coherently, which gives us a better understanding of what happened and why. We begin to feel a sense of control as we process what we experienced from a broader perspective (Newman 2020). It also allows us to connect the dots, making connections we might not have otherwise made, particularly when it comes to uncomfortable thoughts and feelings (Williams 2025). Journaling allows us to externalize those challenging thoughts and feelings, exploring them and thinking about the wider context and implications (Dibdin 2022).

With shadow journaling, reflection is key. This doesn't mean studying it immediately; you're likely to be self-critical if you do this. It would be better to let it sit a bit, and by doing this, you'll probably find that profound insights will emerge all on their own. Some of these realizations won't be comfortable, but that's okay. They are all messengers about important shadow aspects revealing a deeper understanding of your psyche (Williams 2025).

Perhaps you have some journaling experience already, or perhaps you're completely new to it, but either way, you probably haven't journaled with the specific intention of uncovering your suppressed emotions or thoughts before. Choose from these prompts to help you explore your shadow if you don't know where to start (Chan 2023; Clover n.d., Perry 2024):

- List your core values. Do you think you're living by them?
- What situations tend to make you hard on yourself?
- How would you describe yourself? Is it different from how other people would describe you?
- What makes you feel guilty? Is this guilt really yours, or has it been imposed on you by someone else?
- Write about something you're embarrassed to tell other people.
- What situations make you feel like you're not enough?
- Recall a time when you felt triggered by the words or behavior of someone else. Which of your values was being challenged, and what can you learn about yourself from your emotional reaction?
- Recall a time when you judged someone's choice or actions. Which of your values influenced your judgment, and what can your judgment tell you about your values?
- Recall a time when you regretted making a decision. Which of your values were in conflict when you made the decision, and how did this contribute to your regret?
- Think of a time when you felt jealous of someone else's achievements. Which of your values were triggered, and can your feelings of jealousy tell you anything about your own aspirations?
- Do you have any values that you're uncomfortable expressing? Why do you think that is? How might your life be different if you were able to accept and express these values?
- Consider a value that you were conditioned to believe in. Does it genuinely resonate with you, or is it a source of inner conflict? What can you do to resolve this conflict and find out more about your authentic values?

- Do you have any values that have changed over the years? What experiences led to these changes, and how have they affected your choices?
- Are there any parts of yourself that you hide in social situations?
- Are you aware of any patterns in your relationships that make you uncomfortable?
- Do you have any insecurities or fears that are keeping you from following your dreams?
- Are there any experiences from your past that still affect your behaviors or emotions?
- Write about any limiting beliefs or negative self-talk you often engage in. How do you think it affects your decisions and behavior?
- What shadow emotions do you struggle to accept in yourself?
- Are there any parts of you that you're very critical of? How could you be more compassionate to those parts?
- Are there any dreams or deep desires that you ignore? What could you do to change this?
- Write about any self-sabotaging behaviors that undermine your happiness or stand in the way of your success.
- Recall the childhood experiences and conditioning that have molded your beliefs about your self-worth, relationships, and love.
- Write about the coping mechanisms you use to avoid dealing with your emotions.
- Are there any unresolved conflicts or relationships that have had an emotional impact on you? What could you do to heal from these?
- Consider the identities you've adopted in order to be accepted. Do they reflect the most authentic version of yourself?

- Reflect on any recurring dreams or images that come up in your subconscious mind. What messages may they have for you?

Journaling is about being honest with yourself. You don't need to be a brilliant writer—no one will read it but you. Your goal is not to write well—it's to write *real*.

LETTING THE SHADOW BE THE ARTIST

Just like journaling, art doesn't need to be "good" to be useful, and despite the benefits of writing, other forms of art can express things that words can't. Creativity is a powerful healer, and art gives us an alternative way to process our experiences and emotions through the release of energy and self-expression. It's particularly helpful for expressing those emotions that we find difficult to articulate, releasing deeply embedded shadow aspects in the process (The Healing Power of Art and Creativity n.d.).

You don't need any artistic experience to do this. This is about release, not the finished product. The first thing you need to do is choose your medium and gather any equipment you'll need. This can be anything—pick pottery, painting, or make a collage —choose anything you like! You'll need a safe space to practice in; again, the space you've prepared for accessing your inner sanctuary would be ideal, providing you have enough space for your chosen art form.

You'll get the most from this experience if you set your intention first (Creative Journaling + Shadow Work for Beginners n.d.). What do you want to get out of it? Are there any particular themes you'd like to address or a particular change you're hoping to see in yourself? Once you have this clear, you can start exploring. Don't worry; I'll give you some prompts for this too (Sciandra n.d.):

- Explore something that's a deep source of pleasure for you.
- Create something that reflects what you'd do differently in any area of your life if you knew you wouldn't fail.
- Portray an experience, object, or change that you'd like to see in your life.
- If a private detective were following you for a day, what might that person find out?
- Symbolize the moment in the week when you often feel the best, and explore how you feel and why.
- Take a look at something you're avoiding right now.
- Depict what a perfect day that makes you feel peaceful and energized would look like.
- Consider an area of your life in which you're critical of yourself, and show yourself compassion through your art.
- Convey a behavior you engage in that you'd like to change.
- Delve into something you've given up that still lingers in your mind. This could be a passion, a relationship, a job, or anything else that needs closure.
- Express your truth about something you've hidden from others.
- Revisit a moment when you laughed.
- Recollect a moment when you cried.
- Remember a time when something unexpected happened and brought about positive changes in your life.
- Recall a moment when getting what you wanted didn't turn out how you expected it to.

You could also adapt any of the journaling prompts we discussed earlier to suit your artistic exploration and use those—and you don't need to stop at creating your own art either. Engaging with existing art can help you explore your hidden parts, too.

The point is to reflect on art that evokes strong emotions in you or stays with you in some way. When you're moved, it's more likely that the art will trigger your feelings and introspective thoughts. You'll also want to do this in a calm, safe space where you can reflect on the work without being distracted. You may find yourself facing uncomfortable thoughts and feelings, and you want your space to facilitate this. Pay attention to how you react to the artwork, and consider which parts of it are provoking your strongest reactions. Do you notice any themes or recurring images?

It would be a good idea to write all of your reflections down as you go so that you can look back and make associations with your experiences. Just as you did when you were reflecting on your dreams, you want to explore any symbols and archetypes that might give you access to the collective unconscious. Art very often uses symbolism; think about how this is significant to you and what the symbols may be able to tell you about your internal experience. Again, you could use dialogue to facilitate this: Ask yourself what the art wants to tell you about yourself or how it resonates with your experiences. If you feel strong emotions during this process, give yourself permission to feel them fully and express them as you need to, and then let them go. From here, you can evaluate the insights you've discovered and begin to heal and integrate them into your life so that your values and behaviors reflect your true identity (Trovato 2023).

CALM OBSERVATION

I brought mindfulness up briefly in the last chapter, but we're going to explore it a little more closely now. It seems like it's everywhere these days, so don't worry if you have conflicting ideas about exactly what it is—we're going to fix that right now. It's simply the practice of accepting the present moment without judgment—and it's been found to reduce stress and increase our happiness (How to Reduce Stress and Anxiety Through Movement and Mindfulness 2025). To practice mindfulness, you need to be aware of your feelings, thoughts, environment, and sensations in each moment as it unfolds, and you need to let go of any notion that there's a "right" way to feel or think about it (or a "wrong" one for that matter!). It also requires you to let go of all thoughts of the past and future and focus solely on what you're experiencing right now (What Is Mindfulness? n.d.). The idea is to shift your thoughts so that you appreciate the present and gain more perspective.

There has been much research done on the benefits of mindfulness, which include positive changes to both our physical and psychological health. Developing the ability to practice it makes it easier for us to focus on the good things as they happen to us, engage fully in what we're doing, and deal with challenging situations; at the same time, it can reduce stress, improve heart health, reduce pain, and improve sleep (Mindfulness for Your Health 2021). Nevertheless, merely knowing these benefits won't help you: It's good to be aware of them, but it's better simply to practice mindfulness and feel the benefits as they happen. This is an opportunity to embrace curiosity, and this is going to make it much easier to explore your shadow (Mindful Staff 2025). Slowing down your reactions and observing them will show you patterns in your behaviors and thoughts that may be happening on a subconscious level.

I think one of my favorite things about mindfulness is that you can easily fit it into your ordinary life—even when you're not intentionally focusing on your shadow—and this will make it easier to call on mindfulness when you need it. The following are five effortless practices that will help (Pal et al. 2024):

- **Wake up mindfully.** Set up an intentional routine that you can insert into your morning before responsibilities and distractions get in the way. Give yourself five minutes to sit peacefully, breathe deeply, and set your intentions for the day.
- **Eat consciously.** How often do you eat dinner in front of the TV or are otherwise preoccupied when you eat? Mindful eating is about *not* doing this. It's about focusing on your meal, listening to the hunger cues in your body, and giving each bite your full attention. It helps you to pay attention to what your body really needs, and it makes food more enjoyable and satisfying.
- **Make room for the "slow brain."** Most of us are running on autopilot a lot of the time, and we might not even notice every action we take. Take intentional breaks to remind yourself to slow down and pay attention.
- **Work out thoughtfully.** Exercise is an opportunity to focus your mind at the same time as meeting your health and fitness goals. Focus on each moment and coordinate it with your breath to keep yourself focused on the present.
- **Drive mindfully.** Driving is often stressful, but if you approach it kindly and treat both yourself and other drivers compassionately, you'll be able to reduce this and welcome the opportunity for reflection.

Of course, you can also carve time out of your day to practice mindfulness for its own sake. Try this three-minute breathing exercise to get started (Nunez 2023):

1. Set the timer on your phone for three minutes.
2. Sit comfortably in a peaceful space, with your eyes closed if you wish. Pay attention to the sensations in your body and the thoughts running through your mind. Don't judge them; simply observe.
3. Focus on your breath, feeling how the air moves through your body.
4. Extend your focus to your whole body, noticing any areas of tension. Don't try to fight anything; just be.

All the benefits of mindfulness aside, the purpose of practicing it in the context of shadow work is to train yourself to be present with the thoughts and feelings that arise. We're dealing with aspects that may have been hidden in the shadow for a long time, and to identify, express, heal, and integrate them, we need to be able to accept these thoughts and feelings without judgment. Mindfulness will help with this.

3-2-1 SHADOW PROCESS

Our ultimate goal with shadow work is to integrate the parts of ourselves that we've disowned. We can think of these parts as being external to ourselves because we haven't integrated them yet, and as we do this, we'll use a third-person pronoun (3-2-1 Process for the Shadow n.d.).

This process requires you to address your shadow as "it," "she," or "he" to start. Next, you'll address it in the second person—as "you." Finally, you'll talk to it in the first person, as "I." This is because every part of you that has been disowned was at first a part of your first-person awareness. When you buried it in the shadow, you displaced it so that it became a "you"—particularly in cases where you're projecting it onto someone else. If you rejected the aspect so completely that you banished it altogether (so, perhaps, you recognize it as a feeling of fear or rage), it has taken on a third-person status. The 3-2-1 Process is about addressing the shadow at each of these stages in reverse order so that you can ultimately integrate it back into your conscious awareness (The 3-2-1 Process n.d.). This process is most helpful as part of your shadow work regarding projection, but as I mentioned previously, not everything we see in others is necessarily projection. Let's see how this works in practice (Hudson 2025):

1. Pinpoint a situation that triggers you into having a strong emotional reaction. This could also be a person. Describe it/them in detail, giving particular focus to what it is that bothers you. For this stage, you're going to use the third person—e.g., "It makes me feel out of control," or "She's always so dismissive."
2. Now, imagine a dialogue between you and the situation or person you've just described. Ask them questions, and listen to their answers. Now you're going to use the second person—e.g., "What are you trying to show me?" or "Why are you always dismissive of anything I say or do?"
3. Now it's time to own the shadow and move to the first person. Take on the shadow's perspective, and talk as though you are it, expressing its thoughts and feelings and acknowledging it as part of you—e.g., "I do this because I want to be strong, not helpless," or "I dismiss you because I feel unimportant myself." Your goal here is to experience this part of you so that you can heal and integrate it (Jeffrey 2025a).

I want to make this crystal clear, so here's a simplified example. Let's say there's someone in your life who's always falsely confident:

- Third person: "He's full of bravado."
- Second person: "Why do you show bravado all the time?"
- First person: "I feel scared, and it makes me feel more courageous and powerful when I act like this."

By going through this process and shifting your perspective to the first person, you'll begin to own this part of you that has been projected onto others to heal and integrate this shadow aspect into your conscious awareness.

THE GOOD/BAD BOX

How often have you heard the phrase, "She's really nice"? Often, I bet. As children, we're praised for being "good girls and boys," so we've learned to self-identify with traits others hold in high regard. No wonder there's a disconnect between the conscious perception of ourselves and our shadow. As soon as you think that you're a good person, your mind will do everything it can to omit anything you think, do, or say that doesn't match this perception of yourself. It works the other way around, too—if you think of yourself as a bad person, your mind will relegate your positive qualities to the shadow (Jeffrey 2025a).

Let's see this in action. Make a list of every positive quality you see in yourself. Now find the opposite for each one and try to find it inside you. For example, if you identify "self-disciplined" as a quality, you're probably repressing an overindulgent part of yourself. Although exiled to the shadow, this quality is still influencing your attitude and behavior, and because overindulgence has been repressed, it's causing internal tension. If you identify, express, and accept it, you'll be able to bring it back into your conscious awareness. Shadow work confronts the conscious ego, bringing to light the unconscious shadow to integrate the psyche into balance and wholeness (Jeffrey 2025a).

To explore this further, let's turn this into a journaling exercise with these questions (Havekost 2022):

- What part of you do you keep trying to be? What's the opposite of this, and how does it show up in you?
- What don't you like about this aspect of yourself?
- How does this part hurt or offend you?
- How does it hurt or offend other people?
- How does it help or please you?
- How does it help or please other people?
- Why is this part of you important?
- Why do you love this part of you?

We've been through several tools you can use to identify and address your shadow in this chapter, so you're not going to be tackling shadow work unarmed. But these tools aren't enough on their own. The next step is learning how to handle the emotional discomfort and resistance that you're inevitably going to face once the real work begins, and that's what we'll cover in the next chapter.

CHAPTER 6

WHEN THE GOING GETS TOUGH

Emotional avoidance tends to be a response to intense anxiety and fear, and it allows anxiety disorders to persist (Hofmann and Hay 2018). This means that the fear of feeling the anxiety or fear ends up being more harmful than the original feeling, and it's something we can avoid when we have the right tools. When we turn toward discomfort, it's possible to change our response—but, of course, this isn't going to be a comfortable process. In this chapter, we'll explore some of the possible reactions you may experience when you're getting to know your shadow and how to handle the emotions that may arise along the way.

FACING THE HARD

Fear, hesitation, and denial are normal experiences with shadow work. Perhaps you'll notice that you're avoiding journaling, even though you set an intention to do it. Maybe you'll suddenly feel like you're too busy to do the work, or maybe you'll simply feel unmotivated. If you find yourself having any of these reactions, it doesn't mean you're doing it wrong—it means you're getting close to something important. All it means is that you're going to need to release the fear so that you can move forward. I find this process easier to navigate if I break it down into four steps:

Step 1: Identify the belief behind your fear. Somewhere behind what you're feeling is a belief you've held for a long time, and in all likelihood, it originates from a feeling of not being worthy or not being good enough (Smith 2022). Let's say, for example, that you're afraid to look at your bank balance because it doesn't reflect what you want it to. That fear might trigger a lot of related thoughts about what people would think of you if they knew about your financial situation or how you're ashamed to ask for help, even though you know your family would be more than willing to help you. Your mind, in this instance, will most likely go through a range of possible solutions to the problem to get you away from feeling fear, but what will really help you is getting to know more about that fear. If you think back and are willing to sit with the uncomfortable emotion for long enough to explore it, you might find that your fear can be traced back to childhood. Perhaps you were told that money equated to success, and since you're lacking in it, you feel worthless. There we have it. That's the belief behind the fear.

Step 2: As you understand what's causing your fear, you'll probably feel some strong emotions and pain. This energy has been inside you the whole time, and if your goal is to let go of the fear, you must first acknowledge it. Let's go back to our bank balance example—that emotional pain relates to not feeling good enough. You need to have money to believe you're worthy. You might know logically that this isn't true, but fear doesn't care much about logic. To release the fear, you must feel those difficult emotions so that their energy can be processed and released. It's helpful to remember that you're choosing to process your fear and let go of it. This will make you feel safer to feel those emotions (Smith 2022).

Step 3: Replace the belief behind the fear. You can't control what's going on outside you, but you can control what's going on *inside* you. This is what you're doing when you choose to process and let go of the fear. The outside environment will continue to trigger you unless you find a new belief that fits better with what you want—for example, the belief that your self-worth is not defined by external circumstances (Smith 2022). When you're triggered, you'll be able to feel the fear, but instead of letting the emotion take over completely, come back to yourself, remind yourself that you're safe, and affirm your new, aligned belief. Let go of the fear, and feel it exit your body. Breathe in through your nose, hold, and exhale through your mouth (refer to the breathing exercises in Chapter 4 here). Now, you are no longer in survival mode: You're creating the new experience that you desire.

Step 4: Rinse and repeat! Unfortunately, you can't do this once and completely banish your fear forever. Repetition is key to solidifying your new belief, all the while reminding yourself that you have power over your fear. There's no timeline attached to this. You can come back to the process as many times as you need to.

DEFENSE MECHANISMS IN ACTION

There are a few common defense mechanisms that you may notice arising throughout the shadow work process. They may confuse matters somewhat, but what they're trying to do is keep you safe—just as your fear is, even when it doesn't have any logical grounds for doing so. Have you ever found yourself cracking a joke in the middle of a difficult conversation? This is an example of a defense mechanism. You're finding it uncomfortable to have the conversation and feel the tension building, so your defenses kick in and try to lighten the situation with humor. The same thing happens if someone upsets you and you convince yourself that it wasn't really that big of a deal. You don't want to feel upset, so you're minimizing the situation and trying to make yourself feel better.

Defense mechanisms come from the ego, and their goal is to protect your self-esteem (Shadow Work, the Archetypes and Defense Mechanisms n.d.). Many of them are conscious, even if we can't fully admit to what we're doing, but some of them (like repression) are unconscious. Let's explore the most common ones more closely.

Denial

This is a very common defense mechanism, and it happens when you're unwilling to accept facts or reality. You might do this unconsciously by pretending that something didn't happen when other people would be able to tell you that it definitely did (Holland 2022). Your ego is protecting you from pain or discomfort. You see this often in people struggling with addiction. They might deny that they have a problem, even though everyone close to them can see otherwise. The ego uses other defense mechanisms, like projection, along with denial, to keep the difficult emotions from your conscious awareness, so much so that you truly believe the fiction you're creating (Cherry 2024a).

Repression

Repression is similar to denial, but it goes a step further. Difficult emotions, unpleasant thoughts, or painful memories are unconsciously hidden in the hope that you might completely forget them. The problem is, these things don't really go away; they continue to influence your thoughts and behaviors—you just may not know that it's happening (Holland 2022). A good example of this is a survivor of childhood abuse. They may not remember anything about what happened to them, but it continues to affect their relationships, which may trigger painful emotions they can't find a rational reason for (Cherry 2024a).

Projection

We've talked about this one quite a bit already, but it's important to acknowledge that it, too, is a defense mechanism. Instead of recognizing the characteristic as your own, you unconsciously disown it and transfer it onto someone else. This allows the ego to manage the trait more easily, because it believes that the characteristic exists externally rather than within you (Cherry 2024a).

Displacement

This is when you unconsciously direct your emotions, typically anger or frustration, onto an object or another person that doesn't feel like a threat. This means you can react as you wanted to, but now you can do so without risking serious consequences (Holland 2022). We commonly see this in family situations. Perhaps Mom comes home and yells at her husband and kids, not because she's really angry with them, but because she had a bad day. Her subconscious knows that taking her anger out on them will be less of a problem than taking it out on the person it's meant for—a boss or a colleague, for example.

Regression

Sometimes, we might unconsciously revert to an earlier stage of our development when we feel threatened or overwhelmed. This is more obvious in young children. If you've ever known a child who suffered a loss or some other significant trauma, you might have seen them start to act as though they're younger than they are—perhaps they started wetting the bed again, for example, or sucking their thumb, despite having grown out of the habit years ago (Holland 2022). Adults do this too, though—it just isn't always as obvious. You might cry excessively or disproportionately when you receive bad news, chew the end of your pen when you're anxious, or overeat when you're stressed. These are examples of regression to the oral stage of development, when past stress or unmet needs created a fixation. (Cherry 2024a).

Suppression

Usually, we're not conscious of removing thoughts and memories from our awareness (as in the case of repression), but with suppression, we are. Repression isn't a conscious process, but suppression is voluntary: We force the emotion or information out of our conscious mind intentionally (Cherry 2024a). If you've ever chosen not to think about a painful memory or thought and have made a deliberate effort to distract yourself from it and fill your mind with other things, you know a little something about suppression.

Rationalization

This is when you justify or explain a thought, feeling, or behavior that's uncomfortable in a seemingly logical or acceptable way (Cherry 2024a). Rationalization may operate on both the conscious and the unconscious level, depending on the self-awareness of the individual. You might come up with a reason to put your mind at ease, even though a part of you knows that reason isn't actually true (Holland 2022). An example of this is when an unprepared student says a test was unfair or that the teacher hates them instead of admitting to not studying well. It's easy for us to highlight our skills and qualities when we're explaining our successes, but if we're explaining our failures, we're more likely to blame either circumstances beyond our control or someone else (Cherry 2024a).

Sublimation

This is commonly thought to be a more positive strategy than many other defense mechanisms, and it's often done consciously. It occurs when we transform our shadow aspects into an activity that's beneficial. For example, you might take your aggressive tendencies and use that energy toward social activism (Holland 2022). Sublimation is a healthy way to alchemize, ground, and integrate shadow aspects into shadow gold.

Reaction Formation

With this defense mechanism, you don't consciously recognize your socially unacceptable feelings and instead behave in the opposite way (Holland 2022). Reaction formation is sometimes difficult to spot since it appears virtuous on the surface. Additionally, reaction formation can sometimes be confused with suppression—the difference being that suppression is a conscious choice and reaction formation isn't. Moreover, reaction formation is like repression in that both are unconscious, but with repression, the feelings are buried rather than inverted and expressed outwardly. Examples of reaction formation are unknowingly feeling anger deep down, but instead acting in an overly positive way, or being particularly friendly to someone you despise. This defense mechanism is especially counterproductive to shadow integration; it amplifies shadow aspects by exaggerating a lie you've unknowingly sold yourself, ultimately creating more shadow to heal (Cherry 2024a).

Compartmentalization

Compartmentalization isolates conflicting thoughts, feelings, or behaviors in the mind to avoid discomfort. It's mostly unconscious, but it can also be semi-conscious or conscious in certain circumstances. This defense mechanism separates contradicting parts of a person so that they can behave in ways that go against their values, identity, or beliefs without internal conflict. For example, a cheating spouse may box off their guilt and their actions of infidelity and dishonesty into a separate area in their mind to avoid conflict with their moral compass. As related to shadow work, the "compartment walls" must collapse for the different parts of ourselves to be confronted and transformed.

Intellectualization

This is when you deal with a difficult situation by removing emotion from your responses and behaviors, choosing, instead, to focus on objective facts. This defense mechanism is mostly unconscious, but it can also be semi-conscious in those who are self-aware. For example, if you lose your job, you might fill your days with creating documents of job options and potential leads so that you can focus on being proactive rather than feeling the emotions that come with the job loss (Holland 2022). If you receive a frightening diagnosis, you might focus your energy on learning everything you can about the illness and remain as emotionally distant from the situation as possible (Cherry

2024a). In regard to shadow work, these avoided emotions must be acknowledged, felt fully, and then integrated rather than bypassed and disregarded.

You may discover any of these common defense mechanisms during the shadow work process. After all, you're confronting parts of yourself that you've buried deep within your psyche, and addressing them won't always be comfortable. If you recognize any of these defense mechanisms kicking in, breathe, get grounded and centered, and challenge yourself to look deeper to see what's really going on.

YOU DON'T HAVE TO DO THIS ALONE

Shadow work can sometimes stir up more than one person can handle on their own, and this is when you know it's time to ask for help. Pushing through your defense mechanisms is one thing, but there are certain signs that you shouldn't ignore. Be alert to any of the following signals your mind or body is giving you (Heades n.d.; Mental Health Warning Signs and When to Ask for Help n.d.):

- Feeling down for any length of time without knowing the reason for it
- Striking mood changes, swinging between euphoric highs and deep lows
- Constantly worrying about a stressful incident that's already happened
- Difficulty regulating your emotions
- Feeling apathetic
- Feeling persistently overwhelmed or anxious
- Overthinking and feeling like you can't escape your thoughts
- Outbursts of violence or anger

- Difficulty relating to other people's feelings and thoughts
- Suicidal behaviors or thoughts
- Self-harming behaviors
- Experiencing large memory gaps
- Withdrawing from loved ones or social activities
- Having hallucinations, delusions, or sensory experiences that aren't real
- Difficulty breathing, increased heart rate, nausea, or sudden sweating
- Sleeping too little or too much, or feeling fatigued no matter how much sleep you had
- Severe changes in libido or appetite

If you're experiencing consistent problems like any of the above that interfere with your everyday life, it would be a good idea to talk to a friend, coach, or mental health professional. In fact, there are therapists who are very familiar with shadow work, and it may be that you would benefit from working with someone like this. Therapists trained in analytical psychology would be the best people to turn to for this—this might include certified Jungian analysts, therapists training in Jungian analysis, any mental health professional who self-describes as a "Jungian therapist," professionals with links to the C. G. Jung Institute, or therapists who are trained in psychoanalysis (Wigington 2024).

KEEP SHOWING UP

Many of us have a natural instinct to give up when things get uncomfortable. Just think about the number of gym memberships bought with good intentions in the new year that end up unused. But just as with going to the gym, consistency is the secret to getting results. We just have to keep showing up. I think it's important to make the distinction between consistency and intensity here. Let's say you get that January gym membership and go hard five days a week, having not exercised much before that. You're going to become burned out and discouraged very quickly. If, however, you show up twice a week and gradually build up your fitness, you're going to see much better progress in the long run. It's the same with shadow work. The secret isn't to do it intensely in a short period of time; it's to be consistent and accept that change takes time. You don't need to dive deep every day; you simply need to return to the work gently and often.

No bad day on this journey defines you. There will be ups and downs, just as with life. What matters is how you manage those difficult moments, focusing on self-compassion and giving yourself grace. Each step you take to integrate your shadow will help you to build better coping skills, not just for shadow work, but for all aspects of your life. When you're having a challenging day, it's helpful to acknowledge how much progress you've made, to see how far you've come from your starting point. This, in itself, is motivating, especially during those rough spots. Growth and change aren't things that happen overnight. They take time. Remind yourself of that on the more challenging days to help you maintain perspective. Remember why you're doing this, and commit to continuing to show up. Rest when you need to, and ask for help when you need it. Consistency takes commitment, effort, perseverance, and dedication; that's not always easy, but it is all it takes to make progress—no matter what it is you're doing (Rinaldi 2018).

If you're someone who struggles with discipline and consistency, it might help you to train yourself with other habits that aren't so emotionally demanding. Research shows that it takes about 66 days to create a habit (Solis-Moreira 2024), so you might try dedicating a couple of months to learning a new skill or building a habit. Maybe you read for half an hour every day or take up a meditation practice. This will give you faith in your ability to build a new routine, and it will show you the power of consistency, the power of "little and often" (Rivera n.d.).

Of course, you needn't develop a habit that has nothing to do with shadow work—you could simply build small habits that directly relate. I like to think of this as "shadow work lite," bite-sized shadow chunks, if you will, easily digestible with no acid reflux. Over time, it's very powerful. As the proverbs say, Rome wasn't built in a day, but they were laying bricks every hour (John Heywood), and the journey of a thousand miles begins with a single step (Lao Tzu). Perhaps you can spend 15 minutes a day reflecting, checking in on your patterns, or revisiting an insight you've already had. Use the tools in Chapter 5 to help you with this. This is like emotional maintenance—kind of like brushing your teeth—it's the small efforts every day that have a profound and lasting impact.

CELEBRATE!

One thing that will help you keep showing up is taking the time to celebrate your progress—and I don't just mean for the big things. It doesn't matter how small any accomplishment is; celebrating the small wins will still cause your brain to produce dopamine, and this will motivate you to keep going (as well as giving your mood a nice little boost). What you'll end up with is a positive feedback loop that makes you want to keep feeling the satisfaction in your success, and this will help you to keep going. There's another benefit to this, too. When we acknowledge what we've achieved, our brains consolidate the lessons we've been learning along the way (McNally 2024).

Research has found that celebrating small achievements has more impact than waiting to celebrate one big goal—and when you think of it this way, it makes sense (Rothstein and Stromme n.d.). This isn't to say that we shouldn't also celebrate the big wins, though. This brings closure and allows us to recognize the hard work we've put in to get to the moment we're celebrating.

The converse of this is moving on to our next goal without stopping to celebrate the progress we've already made. This can lead to burnout and chronic stress because we keep pushing through without acknowledging what we've already achieved (McNally 2024). It's a sure way to become cynical and down on ourselves—and that's the absolute opposite of what we're trying to achieve here.

So what do we mean by celebrating? It's easy to jump to an image of a big party or drinks with friends when we think about celebration, but your rewards can be much smaller than this. I'd encourage you to make a list of little rewards you can choose from to make it easier (I'll give you a few ideas in a moment) and be clear on your goals so that you notice when you've made progress. For example, you might reward yourself for keeping a dream journal for a week, or you might celebrate recognizing a trait that's been hidden in your shadow. Keep a log of your small victories so that you don't miss them and you can see them adding up. You might even want to tell a friend about them—social support is a powerful thing, especially when it comes to achieving goals, and just because your goal is to get to know, heal, and integrate hidden parts of yourself, it doesn't mean it's any less of a goal than hitting a new personal best at the gym (35 Small Wins to Celebrate This Week 2021).

With all of this in mind, here are a few ideas for rewards you might give yourself to mark your progress (How to Celebrate Small Wins and Make Greater Progress n.d.):

- Take some time out to walk in nature.

- Turn up your favorite music, and sing along.
- Add money to a savings jar that you can later put toward a bigger reward.
- Look at your reflection and congratulate yourself.
- Book a massage or a hair appointment.
- Buy yourself flowers.
- Treat yourself to your favorite meal.
- Make a date with your friends to spend some quality time together.
- Carve out some time to work on a creative project.
- Treat yourself to an activity you enjoy.

There's really no end to what you could do to celebrate, and, at the end of the day, it comes down to what you enjoy and what would feel like a celebration to you. Use one of these ideas, or create your own, or do something else entirely—all that matters is that you take the time to acknowledge your win. Remember, too, that progress doesn't always feel like a breakthrough. Sometimes, it feels like peace. You're going to have to pay attention in order to spot the progress you're making, and that will feed back into your shadow work, which, after all, has a lot to do with self-awareness.

Shadow work isn't just about digging through the dark—it's about making space for more of the good stuff. As you shine a light on your shadow aspects, you'll bring them to light, and, in doing so, you'll create space for more light and find the shadow gold. You'll uncover your unrealized potential and purpose, the sources of your greatest power.

You now know more about how to move through the rough parts, and you know the power of celebration. Now it's time to start noticing what a more integrated life can look like. In Chapter 7, we'll look at what it means to live with more honesty, emotional freedom, and connection to the whole self.

CHAPTER 7
LIVING WHOLEHEARTEDLY

There's another Carl Jung quote I like to remind myself of every now and then: "Wholeness is not achieved by cutting off a portion of one's being, but by integration of the contraries" (McMurrin 2024). In other words, we can't become our whole selves by pretending that the parts we don't like don't exist; we can only become whole by accepting and integrating all of them. Integration, though, isn't a grand finale. It's a quiet return to who we really are, and when we're able to do it, life begins to feel lighter. That's not because life is perfect all of a sudden; it's because it's authentic.

SIGNS THAT IT'S WORKING

You're not going to notice a dramatic change and magically be integrated, but there are some simple, observable signs that will tell you that your shadow work is paying off and you're slowly beginning to shift—and some of them may come as a bit of a surprise, especially the one I'm going to start with: the ability to laugh at yourself. I'm sure that sounds odd, but if you think about it, it's not as strange as it sounds. If you think you have to be perfect and never make mistakes, you still have much work to do; if you can laugh at those mistakes, you're accepting them as part of yourself and looking at them openly (Swerdloff 2024). You're not letting shame or guilt taint your experience. An example of this is a former perfectionist who burns her toast, a mistake she's very familiar with making. What used to send her into a self-deprecating spiral, she's now able to turn into comedy—she laughs and thanks the slice of toast in a eulogy for giving up its life to teach her to lighten up.

You'll also know you're making progress if you notice that you're less reactive, less frequently triggered, or less quick to take offense. As you begin to see the results of your shadow work, your ego won't be as wounded by things that aren't seen as supportive, provoke a memory, or rub up against the scars caused by past events (Swerdloff 2024). When you recognize the progress you've made, however small it is, you'll be motivated to continue the work, accepting that the only way forward is through (Peacock 2023). You'll also be able to acknowledge your own less desirable traits and negative emotions without shame. This is something most of us find hard to do because we only want to feel positive emotions. If we're constantly brainwashing ourselves into thinking that everything's positive just to avoid feeling our authentic feelings (i.e., spiritual bypassing), then there's more shadow work to do. However, when we honor *all* of our emotions, it's a sign that we're beginning to integrate our shadow. We become more self-compassionate, self-reflective, and accepting of who we truly are, contrary emotions and all. We accept that these emotions are ours to manage, finding healthy strategies to help us heal and integrate them rather than banishing them into the shadow or projecting them onto others (Peacock 2023).

Another sign that all your hard work is paying off is when you find it easier to see different perspectives and feel empathy for others. With a broader viewpoint comes understanding and compassion, which then leads to forgiveness. Ultimately, this improves all your relationships—at work, in your personal life, and especially the relationship with yourself (Peacock 2023). It's the rigid and limited ego, one that's not yet integrated with the shadow, that keeps us believing that ours is the only "right" perspective, and as long as it's still running the show, our growth is restricted (Swerdloff 2024). The ego must be dethroned, not destroyed. Being able to accept that there are multiple different answers, paths, and solutions, some of which we may not have thought of ourselves, is a sign that we've been able to balance our ego with other facets of ourselves.

Healing and integration are also evident when we understand other people's opposing viewpoints without letting them manipulate us or giving in to what they want. Instead, we're able to assert ourselves calmly and clearly. We don't need to be angry to lay a boundary, nor do we need to pretend that we're not bothered and allow our hidden emotions to come out in the form of passive-aggression. If we do, it's a sign that there's more shadow work to be done. An integrated shadow will allow us to own our emotional experience fully and use it to guide our actions thoughtfully. We can even handle setbacks with grace and courage, learning from them as we go. We know that things don't always work out exactly the way we want them to, and we're able to take a step back, pivot, and redirect as necessary (Swerdloff 2024).

The signs of progress aren't necessarily loud. More often than not, they're quiet. Take a moment now to reflect on your progress so far. Do you notice any ways in which you've already changed, even if you hadn't realized it before this moment? Really, it comes down to both radical self-awareness and radical self-acceptance. We begin to see ourselves fully and accept ourselves completely, expressing our thoughts and feelings honestly. We become authentic, and authenticity leads to wholeness (Peacock 2023).

WHAT AUTHENTICITY FEELS LIKE

Authenticity isn't about being loud, raw, or confident. It's about not having to filter everything through worries about what other people might think. There's a Jungian concept called "individuation": The idea that we're born with a specific character or unique personality. Individuation is the journey back to our true self, consciously integrating all the parts of our psyche and expressing the whole to the outside world. The reason this can be difficult to achieve is that the world around us doesn't want us to do this; it wants us to stay within the confines of our programming, within specific social, cultural, and political boundaries. Individuation is about finding our way back to ourselves despite the constraints around us, remembering who we truly are and who we were born to be (Farah n.d.).

So, how will you know if you're really being your true self? First off, you'll be more inclined toward curious observation than you are to being reactive. You'll choose not to give your attention to the things that irritate you and, instead, focus your energy on the things (and people) that deserve it. You won't feel that you need to prove anything to anyone—you'll be content with being exactly where you are right now as you figure out what's next, and you can do this while being truly supportive of other people following their own paths. Patterns of self-sabotage will cease, and you'll think carefully about what you can realistically deliver before you make grand promises you can't live up to. Essentially, your words and actions will align, and you'll feel at ease. You'll move more with the flow of life instead of uselessly swimming upstream. This doesn't mean that you won't still experience fear and worry; it's simply that they'll no longer be in control, and you'll see the inner critic as something separate from your authentic self. You'll recognize it as being made up of voices from the past (Govindaraju 2023). Goals and plans will be things you genuinely enjoy pursuing because they're in line with the real, whole you. Whatever you put your energy into will feel meaningful, purposeful, and interesting, reflecting who you truly are. It may challenge you, but this will be something you appreciate rather than something that depletes your energy. You'll care more about your own journey and beliefs instead of shrinking to fit the expectations and desires of others (DePaulo 2021).

You will, however, lose lots of people as you step into your authentic self. These people were acquainted with the unhealed version of you, and many will not resonate with your true self. It may scare people because it challenges their own limiting beliefs about themselves, their own programming, which may make them uneasy about what they see in you as a mirror. As these people pull away, they'll be making room for those who are in alignment with your authentic self. You'll be attracting other people into your circle, people whose journey and energy resonate more with your own (Govindaraju 2023). Your broader perspective and acceptance of your unique journey and experience will help you recognize how this release supports your expansion, and you'll be able to wish those exiting your life well as you let them go, appreciating what they brought for the time that you had them, the lessons, blessings, and all.

Strategies for Developing Authenticity

Shadow work is an ongoing and lifelong process. You may find that you have to revisit the same exercises over and over again to see progress. While you're doing that, however, you can strengthen your authenticity muscles in other ways that will complement the work you're doing with your shadow. One of the simplest and most powerful ways you can do this is to identify your strengths and own them. Are you a great teacher or an excellent listener? Are you good at fixing things? Are you strong or fast? It's not always easy to own our strengths because it feels like it defies social expectations of modesty, but accepting them helps us to become whole. Another way you can become more authentic is by embracing your values. What characteristics and beliefs do you value? Honesty? Integrity? Loyalty? Something else entirely? By naming your strengths and values, you give a voice to qualities that are in alignment with your true self, and it may have a lot to tell you about what you're not embracing right now (Lyons 2021).

What's influencing you from the inside and what's influencing you from the outside also have a part to play in developing authenticity. Other people and social expectations are trying to influence you all the time, and it's important to be able to recognize what's actually important to you when you have all that noise going on around you. What are *your* goals? What do *you* want? Once you have expressed your goals and desires, you can determine why those things are important to you and how they connect you to your purpose. One big indicator of the real you is hidden in your internal dialogue. If you catch yourself telling yourself that you "should" or "ought to" do something, think carefully about those things. Do you think you *should* go for that promotion because you think it's what's expected of you, or do you really want it? You might find more value in asking yourself what your next steps could be rather than getting trapped in a "should" (Lyons 2021).

Pay attention, too, to your emotions. Part of being authentically yourself is being able to recognize your feelings to understand more about who you are. Practice those mindfulness techniques we discussed in Chapter 5 as well, and use journaling as a tool to help you recognize and understand these thoughts and emotions. One thing you may discover as you do this is that fear is more active in your life than you realized, so much so that it might be holding you back from doing the things you'd really like to do. If the stories you tell yourself about why you haven't done something are getting in the way of you actually doing it, it's a sign that you're still being driven by fear, and if that's the case, you're not yet living your authentic life (Lyons 2021).

It's easier to be your true self when those around you are also living their lives authentically. If you haven't found people like this yet, then this is something to prioritize. It may involve putting yourself in new situations that align with your values and expanding outside your comfort zone, but it will be worth it to find the people whose support will help bring out the whole you. Growth happens outside your comfort zone, and hanging on to the parts of yourself that you've kept hidden will keep you from being the most authentic version of yourself. Authenticity takes patience and dedication, and like shadow work, it doesn't happen overnight. It comes along with shadow work, but it, too, must be nurtured in order to support all that work you're doing. Authenticity isn't something you can perform either. Authenticity happens when you *stop* performing —and, chances are, when you get to this point, you'll recognize it right away.

YOUR WORK ISN'T DONE

As I mentioned earlier, shadow work is an ongoing, lifelong process. It doesn't end with one breakthrough; developing a mindset of continuous self-honesty and reflection is key. You're going to have moments of regression, moments where you slip back into old patterns, and you're going to discover new ones that you didn't notice when you first started getting to know your shadow. That's okay. It's all part of the process. Two steps forward, one step back. The trick is to stay connected to your inner world, continuously checking in with yourself and revisiting the exercises you used to get to this point. Here are a few things you can easily integrate into your day so that routine self-check-ins become part of the norm and keep you connected (10 Mindfulness Questions to Help You Check In with Yourself 2024):

- Ask yourself how you're feeling. Name your emotion, and accept it for what it is.
- Ask yourself if there's anything you need to forgive yourself for. If you're holding something against yourself, what could you do to release that burden?
- Focus on something you're grateful for. This can shift your focus onto something genuinely positive without forcing you to create fiction to feel good.
- Find something to celebrate. Remember, every small victory can boost your motivation and self-esteem.
- Identify a thought or a habit that isn't serving you, and imagine releasing it. How could you do this for real, and how would you feel if you did?
- Use a journal to reflect on your feelings and thoughts. Pay attention to whether what you write gives you further insight into your shadow and what aspects of yourself still need to be integrated.

SHARE AND INSPIRE

Inner growth often inspires other people to begin their own journeys, but there's a difference between sharing and preaching. Sharing works best when it's done with humility and consent, and when you do this, it can feed back positively into your own journey. You might think your story isn't important, but if you're open to sharing it with someone else, you may find that you give them the confidence to explore their internal landscape as well. You're giving them a chance to see the real you and inspiring them to find their own authenticity, which will feed back into your personal confidence and self-acceptance (O'Rourke n.d.).

This doesn't mean you should go around advising everyone in your life to do shadow work. That's a conclusion each person has to come to on their own. But what you can do is model what you've learned by being an example and remaining open about what you've discovered about yourself. Consider now whether there might be someone in your life who could benefit simply from seeing you show up more authentically. That's all you need to do. Be the real you.

By this stage in the book, we've moved through discovery, discomfort, and integration—reclaiming energy that used to be scattered or stuck. Now it's time to explore what life can look like when that energy is directed with intention. In our last chapter, we'll explore how reclaiming our shadow aspects leads us to inner strength, clearer purpose, and confident choices.

CHAPTER 8
STEPPING INTO THE LIGHT

I could tell you countless stories about people who've benefited from shadow work, the people who've successfully integrated their shadows and experienced the immense advantages of doing so. Writing a short paragraph about someone you don't know won't do their transformation justice because you won't know what they were like before or how they presented themselves in the world prior to their shadow work journey. You won't see the subtle differences that I have. You won't be able to see the person who picked up music again for the first time in years, or the person who was finally able to assert her boundaries, or the person who started to own his sensitivity and accept his emotional needs. You can hear the stories, but the impact those changes had is much bigger than I can put into words without you knowing their entire process and knowing exactly what those people had hidden inside their shadow.

Your journey, as with the countless others, is about evolution and transformation. You're now stepping into your life as your true self, as someone who has shifted out of old patterns and limiting beliefs into healthier ways of being. This chapter is about how to step into the person you came here to be.

BREAKING WITH THE OLD

Limiting beliefs are the false notions we have that keep us from chasing our desires and goals (Manson n.d.). If you've ever neglected to apply for your dream job or let someone know about your affections for them because you didn't feel like you stood a chance, you know a little something about limiting beliefs. You didn't consciously choose them; you just took them on.

There's more than one type of limiting belief—ones about yourself, the world, or life itself. Some of the beliefs that have the greatest impact on us are those we hold about ourselves. These are the ones that can hold us back the most. Let's take the example of someone who believes that they're hard to love or unworthy of love. Perhaps the reason for this comes from abandonment or repeated rejection in childhood or relationships, or from caregivers who were emotionally distant, critical, or hot-and-cold with affection. The real cause could very well be that they were loved poorly by those who couldn't see their worth or couldn't give them healthy love because they didn't even know how to love themselves. The beliefs we hold about ourselves are filled with personal insecurities and emotional attachments, and this makes them challenging (but not impossible) to transform.

Our limiting beliefs about the world around us are perhaps slightly less damaging to our self-image, but they're still impactful. An example is the belief that other people can't be trusted, and you can't trust yourself either, because you trusted them in the first place. Generalizing all people based on a few bad experiences closes you off from fulfilling relationships, prevents you from connecting with others, and creates a defensive mindset. Because you're afraid of being betrayed or disappointed, you'll then block opportunities from yourself. You can catch these limiting beliefs quite easily if you pay attention to your internal monologue. If you're thinking about doing something and the first thought that comes to mind has to do with how other people might judge you or you're second-guessing yourself, you've found one. The truth is, not all people are unsafe, and although some have harmed you, others have shown you kindness and integrity. You can keep your heart open while still practicing discernment and self-love.

Interestingly enough, your beliefs about the world can go the other way, too. Generally, our limiting beliefs have us seeing ourselves through a negative lens in some way, but sometimes we can be overly positive about ourselves, sometimes to the point of delusion (Manson n.d.). An example might be a musician who doesn't put themselves forward because they think no one will appreciate their eclectic tastes, or a budding entrepreneur who doesn't follow through with a business idea because they think no one will understand their vision. The idea that they're special and they won't get what they deserve holds them back before they even try.

The final type of belief that can limit us is one that we hold about life in general—about what life's supposed to look like. A good example of this is when we think that we've missed an opportunity because someone else has already done it. Perhaps you want to start a new business but discover that someone else "beat you to the punch," so you drop the idea completely—but what if you could have competed with them and used the experience to improve upon your vision? Or maybe you're looking for a new relationship, and you decide that everyone your age is already taken. Firstly, who said your partner has to be exactly the same age as you, and secondly, how do you really know if you don't even look? In both cases, it's your limiting beliefs about life that are holding you back.

Another good example is thinking that if life hasn't worked out for you by now, it means it probably never will. Perhaps you believe you're too old, too broken, or too late. You might even claim that things are impossible, so you never try them and risk failure. Perhaps these beliefs come from continuously being disappointed by things not going your way, seeing others succeed while you stumble, or societal or cultural pressures for financial success, marriage, starting a family, etc. But life unfolds in its own time, and as long as you have a pulse, it's never too late to become who you're destined to be. If you don't open yourself up to the possibilities because you're afraid of failing, though, you'll never know.

When we hold onto these constricting beliefs, we let the ego keep us safely within our comfort zones. Sometimes, this happens because we've unconsciously built up defense mechanisms to protect ourselves from being hurt in the same ways we've been hurt in the past (Wooll 2022). This is something you may uncover through your shadow work, and you may find that it's behind your anxiety, tendency to procrastinate, or impostor syndrome. To challenge any limiting belief, we need to know where it came from in the first place, and there are three likely suspects (Wooll 2022):

- **The family values you were brought up with.** Our core beliefs start to develop very early in life, and we learn them from our families, even when they're not intentionally taught. They could be about anything from career paths to beliefs about different kinds of people, and they will influence you for the rest of your life unless you address them.

- **Your life experiences.** These are the ones that tend to get stuck in the shadow. Every experience you have leaves you with a feeling that your subconscious remembers, and this will influence your beliefs and behaviors moving forward.
- **Your education.** Just as your family values influenced your core beliefs, so, too, did the beliefs passed on to you by your teachers and friends. Anyone whose job was to share information with you had the power to influence you, and if you had a lot of respect for them, you're even more likely to believe anything they told you. These beliefs can stick with you whether they're objectively true or not.

CHALLENGING A LIMITING BELIEF

How, then, do we challenge these limiting beliefs? Not surprisingly, the place to start is to identify them. If you think you may have several, take it one belief at a time, starting with the biggest one (Miranda n.d.). This won't necessarily be easy. Often, these beliefs have become so ingrained in us that we don't even know we have them. I like Descartes' take on this. He realized that since everything he thought he knew came through his senses (which can sometimes be deceiving), he couldn't know whether or not it was true without testing it. He began to reject each thing he thought he knew, allowing back in only the beliefs he was certain were true. This is where the famous phrase, "I think, therefore I am," came from: The one thing he was absolutely certain of was that he existed (Roache 2022). Descartes' approach, while a little extreme for what you need to do here, gives us a good framework for identifying those limiting beliefs. If you're struggling to find them, try brainstorming "facts" you think you know about yourself and the world, considering how you know them to be facts. You may find that some of them aren't as true as you originally thought.

Next, figure out where the belief came from. No matter how objective we try to be, we're always viewing the world through a filter. If you're looking at something you created, for example, whether it's a painting, a piece of writing, or a cake, what you see has more to do with you and your relationship with that creation than it does with its objective reality. The way you see it is filtered through your beliefs about yourself, the world, and life in general. With the belief you identified in the last step, ask yourself where it came from. Is it something you can trace back to your childhood or a particular life experience? Is it a message you've received from society or the culture you were brought up in? Remind yourself that this belief is just a belief; it's not a fact.

Once you have an idea about where it came from, ask yourself if it's still true for you. I'd recommend exploring this through writing rather than thinking about it in your head. Our beliefs and ideas are often only partially formed, and this makes it hard to find the flaws in them. Write your belief down so that you understand it better, and you may immediately see that it has little basis in fact. Few of us articulate our limiting beliefs, probably because they make us uneasy, which means we've never allowed ourselves to see their flaws (Roache 2022). Ask yourself whether this belief is truly founded in reality, and determine if your explanation makes sense. Do you have any facts to support it? Did you always have this belief, and if not, what changed and when? Can you find any evidence that contradicts it? Now ask yourself what it would be like if you believed differently. How would you benefit? What you're doing here is expanding your perspective so that you may alter the belief (Miranda n.d.).

The next thing to do is try out a different filter. To do this, you're first going to have to let go of the idea that there's any one "right" way to let reality in. You're still going to be looking at it through a filter; it just isn't going to be the same one you're familiar with using. You can play with this idea at first until you become more comfortable with it. Let's say you don't believe you're as smart as your colleagues. Try to imagine what it would be like if you believed you were just as smart as they are. Would your attitude toward work change? Would you do anything differently? If nothing else, this exercise will show you how your beliefs affect your attitudes and decisions and how changing them may create new possibilities you've never even imagined (Roache 2022).

While you're looking at your personal belief from different perspectives, ask yourself whether you'd believe the same about someone else. Would you believe that your friend wasn't as smart as his colleagues? Probably not. You'd tell him to go for the promotion he was hesitating to apply for because he thought he wasn't smart enough, and even if he didn't get an offer, the last thing you'd say was that he was right all along. By doing this, you can identify whether a double standard exists and, if so, reject it.

All in all, you're still human, so give yourself some grace throughout this process. Even if you recognize your belief as false, it can still influence you. Your feelings won't change overnight, so be gentle with yourself. You may also have to work on some of your character traits to change your beliefs. For example, if you have a limiting belief that keeps you from asking for help, focus on becoming less militantly self-reliant, while giving yourself plenty of time to integrate and adjust (Roache 2022).

Your beliefs *can* change, but only once you see them clearly. Starting with your biggest limiting belief, work through these steps to challenge it, and if there are many, continue the process for each. Rewrite that belief so that it's no longer limiting: Change it into something empowering instead, something that will truly serve you on your journey.

USING THE SHADOW

The energy that you've used to suppress parts of yourself is now available for something better. Earlier on, we talked about how anger can be used constructively, and this is a good example to bring up at this point. Many of us express our anger unproductively or repress it entirely, but we can teach ourselves to use it for safety and empowerment instead. We can do that by using anger to set boundaries and to reinforce those boundaries as often as necessary when they're violated. Accessing your anger to keep those boundaries sacred and refusing to stay silent to avoid conflict reflects what you're unwilling to accept. If you've been conditioned to value the wants and needs of others more than your own values, chances are, you've probably locked your anger away in the shadow. Once you have access to it and are able to wield it in productive and healthy ways, it becomes a useful tool for boundary setting and reinforcement.

To develop a healthy relationship with anger, pay attention to the feeling of it rising, which, you'll find, often points to one of your boundaries being crossed. That anger is indirectly telling you to take action to protect your boundary, and when you listen, you're not only helping yourself; you're also teaching others how to treat you. When anger is used as a guide instead of as a weapon, it's more manageable, and this often means you're less likely to act in a counter-productive or disrespectful way (Moore 2018).

Jealousy can be used constructively, too. It can be used as a tool for introspection and self-honesty. Let's say you're jealous of your partner's relationships with others. What's this jealousy trying to tell you? Are you insecure? Is there an underlying fear of abandonment? Do you feel powerless and have a desire to gain control? Is there cultural or societal shame about expressing your emotional needs? Once you've identified the cause or causes, you can have a healthy, open-hearted, and honest conversation with your partner about why you're jealous. Focus on your own concerns rather than blaming them for their actions, and be prepared for them to have their own emotional response. What you're doing now is using jealousy as a tool for a conscious conversation, and this will allow you to clarify the boundaries of your relationship. Ultimately, this will make both of you feel safe, seen, and heard (Wisner 2023).

Fear, meanwhile, can be turned into preparation. After all, the level of fear you have is often related to how prepared you feel about a particular situation. It stands to reason that the more prepared you are, the less fearful you'll become. To do this, identify your fear and describe the worst-case scenario in writing so that you can see exactly what's making you afraid. Now, come up with a plan for how you'd deal with the worst-case scenario if it happened. It's unlikely that it will, so you only need to prepare and plan enough to put your mind at ease (Waschenfelder n.d.). For example, if your fear relates to swimming in open water, your worst-case scenario might be that you'll get swept away by a current and drown. You don't need to come up with a plan for every stage of this scenario because it's very unlikely to happen, but if you tell yourself that you'll swim with a life jacket and make sure there's always someone watching you, this should be enough to reduce your fear.

Negativity can be seen through a positive lens, just as negative emotions can be used as a catalyst for positive change. For example, if you're disgusted by the once-beautiful shoreline in your hometown that now looks like a dump site, you can turn this disgust of neglect and pollution into local environmental activism. Instead of feeling disgust, wouldn't you like to feel proud of your hometown? Perhaps you'll decide to lead a clean-up effort or advocate for local ordinances or initiatives. Here, you're turning a negative emotion into positive action, which, over time, will lead to more positive emotions and outcomes because it will transform other negatives into positive energy (Stockwell 2022).

As a society, we're biased toward happiness, so it's very tempting to suppress negative emotions, even though they're an integral part of the human experience. We think we should always feel good, so we pretend the negative doesn't exist, but by doing so, we dishonor our true feelings and indirectly feed more into the negative. Research has found that people who chase happiness tend to be less happy than those who don't because of the discrepancy between how they feel and how they think they should feel (Subramaniam 2022).

We'd be better off acknowledging and processing our negative emotions: Every one of them is worth experiencing, and every one of them can be channeled into something positive if we make that conscious choice. We can also choose to feel them, listen to their message by bearing witness to them, and then let them go. Negative emotions are here to guide us; they have positive lessons to teach us. When things seem hopeless, it often means that there's an opportunity to turn a situation or perspective around, so take advantage of the learning opportunity and focus on what you want rather than on what you don't want. Your negative emotion is a messenger for your true desires (Tumanishvili n.d.). Your shadow is fuel, not baggage, and the parts that you once kept hidden from yourself are valuable inner resources: They're your shadow gold.

BOUNDARIES AND CHOICES

Real empowerment shows up when you make clear choices: when you say yes, when you say no, when you stand firm, and when you walk away. This all has to do with boundaries. Whenever you decline something you don't want to do, express your feelings or experiences honestly, make your expectations clear, or address a conflict directly, you're working within healthy boundaries. To set a boundary, you'll need to be as clear and direct as you can be without needing to raise your voice. Say what it is you require or desire (without saying what you don't like), and be prepared to feel some uncomfortable emotions like guilt or remorse (Nash 2018). You might not yet be used to setting healthy boundaries or putting your needs first, so until you are, there may be echoes from your past self still coming through, or a caretaker's voice saying that it's not a very nice thing to do. Remember, your emotions are trying to tell you something: If you feel guilt or remorse about putting your needs first, perhaps there's a lesson to be learned about honoring yourself more. When you're laying a boundary with someone, make sure you're specific and the conversation isn't rushed. You should both be able to focus on the conversation without distractions (Reid 2025).

No matter how well you set your boundaries, there will always be times when someone will cross a line, accidentally or not. If this happens, express your boundary again, and lay down a consequence for repeated boundary violations. If, for example, you've laid a boundary about taking turns in conversation with someone who has a habit of interrupting, you might say something like, "If it happens again, I will have to end the conversation for now." You should only do this, however, if you're willing to follow through with the consequence; otherwise, you'll be teaching the other person that you're not serious about your own boundaries (Reid 2025).

It's not always easy to assert or maintain your boundaries when you're used to people-pleasing or conflict avoidance. If this is the case for you, try asking yourself these questions to help you stay in alignment (Raveling 2012; Yaw n.d.):

- Is this a priority for me? Is what you're considering agreeing to in alignment with your needs and desires, or would you be doing it for someone else?
- What's really important to me? This may take you a while to figure out if you're used to putting everyone else before yourself.
- How will I feel if I say yes (or no)? You're not considering anyone else here, only yourself. You can't make everyone happy, so you may as well start by making yourself happy.
- What is the other person expecting of me? Are you realistically able to do it without making sacrifices that will hurt you?
- Can I still care about this person without doing exactly what they want me to?
- How would I deal with this situation if I wasn't worried about making this person happy?

RESILIENCE ISN'T ALWAYS LOUD

Being resilient is about having the ability to face difficulties without reverting to unhealthy coping strategies or shrinking away. It's your internal reservoir of strength, something you can draw on to deal with and bounce back from challenges (Cherry 2024b). It's emotional flexibility, and you're already probably more resilient than you believe.

The five key pillars of resilience are strong social connections, good problem-solving skills, emotional regulation, self-compassion, and survivor mentality (Cherry 2024b). With strong social connections, you have people around you who can help you handle difficulties, and this is critical to your emotional resilience (Brown 2025). Good problem-solving skills, meanwhile, give you the ability to find logical and sometimes creative solutions. They also make you less likely to fall into the trap of tunnel vision, which means you'll be more able to navigate a situation toward your desired outcome (Cherry 2024b). Emotional regulation is about recognizing when you're having an emotional response to a situation and managing those emotions so that you can deal with the practicalities calmly. Bonus points if you can also extend compassion toward yourself—when you need to take a break, accept your emotions as they arise, and treat yourself kindly as you deal with the situation. Lastly, survivor mentality is an empowerment shift that will take away from victim mentality so that you're more likely to look for solutions instead of other people to blame (Cherry 2024b).

If you're concerned that you may still be lacking in any of these areas, don't worry. There are things you can do to develop your emotional resilience. Here are my favorites (Barker 2016; Webb Wright 2023):

- **Work on your growth mindset.** Your emotional resilience shouldn't be measured against anything other than your own meter, so try not to compare yourself to others. Let go of mistakes you've made in the past, and focus on what you can do now. Your skills can improve if you commit to learning from your mistakes rather than using them to judge yourself.

- **Set boundaries that protect your time and energy.** A big part of resilience is being comfortable with disappointing people every once in a while in order to focus on your own needs. Sometimes we just have to put ourselves first.
- **Work on your ability to regulate your emotions.** You're still going to feel difficult emotions, but if you're aware of them, you'll be able to redirect and manage them just as we discussed earlier.
- **Accept that you're not perfect.** Just like everyone else, you're going to make mistakes. A mark of resilience is when you're able to keep imperfections from ruining your day and adapt to changing circumstances, even when it's not quite what you were hoping for.
- **Make time for self-care.** You need fresh air, exercise, time with the people you love, and alone time. A lot of us fall into the trap of thinking that taking time to prioritize self-care is selfish, but it isn't. It's absolutely necessary. If you're exhausted and stretched too thin, your resilience will take a hit, and you won't be able to show up for others to the best of your ability.
- **Write about your feelings.** It seems like journaling is recommended for everything these days, but it really does help you to regulate your emotions and work through your problems, which, ultimately, increases your emotional strength.
- **Celebrate all your successes—even the little ones.** Focus on what you're doing right rather than on your mistakes. If you don't lose your temper in a stressful moment, that's something to be proud of. If you find an alternative solution to a problem after making a mistake, that's something to be proud of. Give yourself credit for becoming a stronger person, and it will feed back into that resilience.

- **Be willing to ask for help.** Many of us have been conditioned to think that asking for help is a sign of weakness, but it's quite the opposite. Resilient people don't worry about what other people think of them, and asking for support helps them to build better social connections.
- **Welcome change.** Heraclitus said that the only constant in life is change (King 2019), and although it's not always comfortable, often, good things come from it. Change gives you the opportunity to learn new things and fuel your personal growth.
- **Confront your problems.** Just as change is inevitable, sometimes bad things happen. Avoiding problems isn't healthy, but when we accept them, we're more equipped to adapt and find solutions.
- **Build healthy relationships.** Everyone needs supportive people to talk to and trust to give them honest feedback. Strong connections help us remain solid and grounded.
- **Broaden your perspective.** When you're able to see things from another person's perspective and realize that there may be more than one right answer to the same problem, your resilience increases.
- **Practice gratitude.** One of the best things you can do when something doesn't go your way is to focus on the things you're grateful for. If you look back at every small part of your day, you'll find lots of things to be thankful for, even if they're very small. The more ingrained this practice becomes, the easier it will be to pick yourself up after something goes wrong because you'll be aware of all the good things in your life.
- **Reframe your negative thoughts.** When they're running through your mind all day, negative thoughts prevent you from feeling positivity. Try to catch these

thoughts as they arise and reframe them immediately. For example, if the thought that comes to mind is, "I'm really bad at this," you might reframe it to say, "I'm getting better at this."
- **Maintain a positive outlook.** This doesn't mean you need to see the world through rose-tinted glasses, but if you're able to look at it with a realistic yet optimistic outlook, you're going to find it easier to overcome challenges and keep yourself in a positive frame of mind.
- **Face your fears.** When you avoid the things that scare you, you're only going to become more afraid of them. It's only when you face them that your fears become less frightening.
- **Be flexible.** Resilient people are flexible in the way they react to stress and approach challenges. Much like how the same coping mechanism won't work in every situation, being flexible in the way you think about problems will make it easier to overcome them.

THE FUTURE YOU CHOOSE

I want to ask you, now, to envision a future in which your actions are guided by clarity and courage rather than confusion and fear. To help you with this, I'm going to guide you through a short visualization exercise. I recommend that you record yourself reading it out loud so that you can listen to it (Envisioning Your Future, Pt. III—Future Self Visualization 2024):

Sit somewhere comfortable, close your eyes, and breathe slowly and deeply as you relax your mind and body. Imagine yourself traveling upward above your chair, over your home, your city, and your coun-

try, and up through the clouds until you're in space. Envision a beam of light taking you back to Earth 20 years in the future. Look around you and notice your home. This home belongs to your future self. What does it look like? What do you look like? What are you wearing? What's your energy like, and how are you feeling? Have a conversation with this future version of you. Ask yourself what's stood out the most to you in the last 20 years. What dreams have come true? What have you achieved? Ask yourself how you get from where you are now to where you are 20 years in the future. What advice do you have for yourself?

Before you leave, thank this future version of you for your wisdom, and remind yourself that you can visit any time you like. Travel back up through the beam of light that brought you here, back into space, and back down through the clouds, into your country, your city, and your home, until you settle softly back down in your chair. Gently open your eyes, and focus on your breathing for a few moments until you're fully back in the present.

Give yourself a few minutes after completing this visualization exercise to reflect on what you learned from your future self. What feelings, thoughts, and possible next steps come up for you? It's possible that in the coming days, you might have a clearer idea of how to get to where you want to go or more determination to take the necessary steps to get there. You might see how your current actions and behaviors are impacting your long-term goals and change your ways to bring these ambitions to fruition. Allow this future version of you to guide you toward your destiny!

Shadow work isn't about perfection. It's about showing up fully —messy, honest, and strong enough to be seen. Now that you've healed and integrated the parts of yourself that were once hidden, you have access to deeper truths, broader choices, and a greater sense of peace. What comes next is for you to create—manifesting now, not through fragmentation, but as your highest expression of self.

CONCLUSION

How do you feel now that you've met your whole self? The process isn't always comfortable, but nearly everyone I've worked with has told me that they ended up feeling happier about who they are now than they felt when they began their shadow work journey. Reclaiming the parts of themselves that were hidden in the shadow for so long was integral to their wholeness and seeing themselves honestly.

I hope that you're feeling the benefits too, but there's still a long journey ahead of you. Remember that shadow work is a lifelong process, and you may have to revisit the exercises in this book many times. You're going to continue experiencing life, and this means that there'll be plenty of opportunities for your subconscious to bury more things in the shadow. This is natural, and all it means is that your self-awareness must be ever-present. Be prepared to meet your shadow again, and be ready to face the parts of you that are getting hidden away. The process gets easier over time because you're a more authentic version of yourself who knows yourself better.

Perhaps you decided to read this book cover-to-cover before you began your shadow work. That's okay too, but now it's time for your work to begin. Start small, but start now. A life that feels more like home doesn't show up by accident. It shows up when the shadow is finally welcome at the table. It's not a guest at your table, though; it's part of you—part of your whole, authentic self, and it deserves its seat just as much as every other part of you does.

You're prepared now for a truly fulfilling future, one that meets your needs, inspires you, and fills you with joy and peace. You are your authentic self. You are whole. Embrace your shadow as warmly as you embrace the future: You're deserving, and it's only when you do this that you'll finally live your truth. Thank you for accompanying me on this journey. It's been an honor and a blessing to walk with you.

SHARE YOUR EXPERIENCE!

Everyone's on their own path, but you can do more to help other people on their journey to wholeness than you might think. Share your experience and introduce others to the concept of shadow work, and I'm sure you'll inspire them. You can also help people you'll never meet—just by leaving a short review.

Simply by sharing your honest opinion of this book and a little about your own experience with shadow work, you'll inspire other people to get to know their own hidden parts and discover what it means to live as their most authentic self.

Thank you for healing not only yourself but also the world around you.

Scan the QR code to leave your review.

REFERENCES

Aburrow, Yvonne. 2021. "The Golden Shadow." Dowsing for Divinity, November 11. https://dowsingfordivinity.com/2021/11/11/the-golden-shadow/.

"The Active Imagination Technique: Essential Steps for Creative Exploration." 2019. Envision Your Evolution, June 26. https://www.envisionyourevolution.com/analytical-psychology/active-imagination-technique-essential-steps/2432/.

"Addressing the Self: The Importance of Self-Awareness for Healing." n.d. Driftwood. Accessed July 11, 2025. https://driftwoodrecovery.com/blog/addressing-the-self-the-importance-of-self-awareness-for-healing.

Adonis, Marios, Marina Loucaides, Mark J. Sullman, and Timo Lajunen. 2025. "The Protective Role of Self Compassion in Trauma Recovery and Its Moderating Impact on Post Traumatic Symptoms and Post Traumatic Growth." *Scientific Reports* 15 (1). https://doi.org/10.1038/s41598-025-91819-x.

Alexander, Jenny. 2012. "It's 'the Seat of Creativity' – So How Can You Find Your Shadow?" *Jenny Alexander's Blog* (blog), November 8. https://writinginthehouseofdreams.com/2012/11/08/it-is-the-seat-of-creativity-so-how-can-you-find-your-shadow/.

Bagga, Aadrika, Julia Barro, Shai Kanow, Tamara Ratkovic, Nil Sarper, Radhika Soni, and Nini Walters. 2024. "From Childhood to Adulthood: The Impacts of Trauma on Anxiety Disorders." *OxJournal*, September 16. https://www.oxjournal.org/from-childhood-to-adulthood-the-impacts-of-trauma-on-anxiety-disorders.

Barker, Eric. 2016. "10 Ways to Boost Your Emotional Resilience, Backed by Research." *Time*, April 26. https://time.com/4306492/boost-emotional-resilience/.

Biesalski, Conni. 2021. "The Essential Guide to Shadow Work: Integrate Your Wounded Parts + Live Your Authentic Self." *Conni Biesalski* (blog), May 10. https://www.conni.me/blog/shadow-work.

Birk, Abby. n.d. "Guided Visualization Meditation to Build a Sense of Safety." Riverbank Therapy. Accessed July 11, 2025. https://www.riverbanktherapy.com/blog/2023/12/14/guided-visualization-meditation-to-build-a-sense-of-safety.

Brandon, Nathan. 2022. "Jungian Dream Analysis: Exploring the Unconscious Mind." Dr Nathan Brandon, March 10. https://drnathanbrandon.com/jungian-dream-analysis-exploring-the-unconscious-mind/.

"Breathing Exercises for Stress." 2022. NHS, August 15. https://www.nhs.uk/mental-health/self-help/guides-tools-and-activities/breathing-exercises-for-stress/.

Brown, Lachlan. 2025. "8 Signs You're More Emotionally Resilient Than 98% of People, Says a Psychologist." *Personal Branding Blog* (blog), January 24. https://personalbrandingblog.com/dan-signs-youre-more-emotionally-resilient-than-98-of-people-says-a-psychologist/.

REFERENCES

Calinawan, Jonah. 2020. "How to Analyze a Dream Using Jungian Dream Analysis." *Jonah Calinawan* (blog), July 17. https://jonahcalinawan.com/blog/jungian-dream-analysis/.

Campbell, Farrah. 2019. "Using Curiosity to Find Your Best Self." *Stackery* (blog), February 13. https://www.stackery.io/blog/using-curiosity/.

"Carl Jung and the Psychology of Dreams—Messages from the Unconscious." 2023. Academy of Ideas, June 20. https://academyofideas.com/2023/06/carl-jung-and-the-psychology-of-dreams-messages-from-the-unconscious/.

Carter, Samantha. n.d. "How to Create an Inner Sanctuary: Designing Spaces for Mental Health and Well-Being." Plus by APN. Accessed July 11, 2025. https://plusapn.com/resources/condition/how-to-create-an-inner-sanctuary/.

Chan, Katharine. 2023. "50 Shadow Work Prompts for Your Next Journal Session." Psychedelic Support, August 28. https://psychedelic.support/resources/50-shadow-work-journal-prompts/.

Chan, K.M., and K. Horneffer. "Emotional expression and psychological symptoms: A comparison of writing and drawing." *The Arts in Psychotherapy* 33, no. 1 (2006), 26-36. doi:10.1016/j.aip.2005.06.001.

Cherry, Kendra. 2024a."20 Defense Mechanisms We Use to Protect Ourselves." *Verywell Mind*, March 6. https://www.verywellmind.com/defense-mechanisms-2795960.

Cherry, Kendra. 2024b. "What Resilience Means (and Why It Matters)." *Verywell Mind*, September 29. https://www.verywellmind.com/characteristics-of-resilience-2795062.

Cherry, Kendra. 2024c. "What You Should Know About the Oedipus Complex." *Verywell Mind*, June 26. Accessed July 11, 2025. https://www.verywellmind.com/what-is-an-oedipal-complex-2795403.

Cherry, Kendra. 2025. "How to Understand and Identify Passive-Aggressive Behavior." *Verywell Mind*, January 30. https://www.verywellmind.com/what-is-passive-aggressive-behavior-2795481.

Childs Heyl, Julia. 2023. "Inner Child Work: How Your Past Shapes Your Present." *Verywell Mind*, March 22. https://www.verywellmind.com/inner-child-work-how-your-past-shapes-your-present-7152929.

Clear, James. n.d. "Rome Wasn't Built in a Day, But They Were Laying Bricks Every Hour." James Clear. Accessed July 12, 2025. https://jamesclear.com/lay-a-brick.

Clover, Molly. n.d. "25 Shadow Work Journal Prompts to Discover Your True Self." Molly Clover. Accessed July 11, 2025. https://mollyclover.com/25-shadow-work-journal-prompts-to-discover-your-true-self/.

Colwell, Maggi. 2024. "The Truth About Shadow Work and Carl Jung." Chiron Art Therapy, February 26. https://columbusarttherapy.com/the-truth-about-shadow-work-and-carl-jung/.

Copley, Laura. 2024. "12 Jungian Archetypes: The Foundation of Personality." *PositivePsychology.com*, April 8. https://positivepsychology.com/jungian-archetypes/.

"Creative Journaling + Shadow Work for Beginners." n.d. Pixel Park. Accessed July 11, 2025. https://thepixelpark.com/creative-journaling-shadow-work-for-beginners/.

Deaver, Diana. 2020. "A Depth Psychological Exploration of Ego and Shadow." Emotional

REFERENCES 135

Health Coaching, February 16. https://emotionalhealthcoaching.com/depth-psychology-ego-shadow/.

DePaulo, Bella. 2021. "How to Know That You're Living Authentically." *Psychology Today*, July 12. https://www.psychologytoday.com/us/blog/living-single/202107/how-to-know-that-youre-living-authentically.

Dibdin, Emma. 2022. "The Mental Health Benefits of Journaling." *Psych Central*, March 31. https://psychcentral.com/lib/the-health-benefits-of-journaling.

Drymalski, Andy. n.d. "Jungian Psychology Series: The Shadow." Jungstop. Accessed July 11, 2025. https://jungstop.com/jungian-psychology-series-the-shadow/.

Elsass, Chloe. 2021. "Befriending My Shadow: The Power of Active Imagination." Elephant Journal, June 24. https://www.elephantjournal.com/2021/06/befriending-my-shadow-the-power-of-active-imagination-chloe-elsass/.

"Envisioning Your Future, Pt. III—Future Self Visualization." 2024. Athena Wellness, February 15. https://athenawellness.com/blog/2024/2/15/envisioning-your-future-pt-3-future-self-visualization.

Fairbank, Rachel. 2021. "How to Identify Your Shadow Emotions (and Why You Should)." Lifehacker, October 25. https://lifehacker.com/how-to-identify-your-shadow-emotions-and-why-you-shoul-1847897185.

Farah, Stephen. n.d. "Towards Authenticity." Center of Applied Jungian Studies. Accessed July 12, 2025. https://appliedjung.com/towards-authenticity/.

"15 Journal Prompts for Self-Compassion." 2021. *Dreaming by Dusk* (blog), May 21. https://www.dreamingbydusk.com/blog/journal-prompts-for-self-compassion.

Fletcher, Jenna. 2024. "How to Use 4-7-8 Breathing for Anxiety." *Medical News Today*, August 21. https://www.medicalnewstoday.com/articles/324417.

Frye, Devon. 2021. "Why It's OK to Share Your Success." *Psychology Today*, January 5. https://www.psychologytoday.com/us/articles/202101/why-its-ok-share-your-success.

Garoutte-Mohammed, Grace. 2024. "What Is Shadow Work? Definition and Prompts to Get Started." *BetterUp* (blog), December 23. https://www.betterup.com/blog/shadow-work.

Gee, Dylan G. 2020. "Caregiving Influences on Emotional Learning and Regulation: Applying a Sensitive Period Model." *Current Opinion in Behavioral Sciences* 36 (December): 177–184. https://doi.org/10.1016/j.cobeha.2020.11.003.

Gerbrandt, Nathan. n.d. "The Power of Shifting Judgement to Curiosity." Crisis & Trauma Resource Institute. Accessed July 11, 2025. https://ctrinstitute.com/blog/the-power-of-shifting-judgement-to-curiosity/.

Gooden, Kelsey. n.d. "The Dos and Don'ts of Shadow Work Journaling." Little Infinite. Accessed July 11, 2025. https://www.littleinfinite.com/the-dos-and-donts-of-shadow-work-journaling/.

Govindaraju, Rashmi. 2023. "8 Obvious Signs You Are Living Your Most Authentic Life." *Medium*, October 27. https://medium.com/illumination/8-obvious-signs-you-are-living-your-most-authentic-life-f9c33547308a.

REFERENCES

"Grounding Strategies." n.d. The University of Arizona. Accessed August 11, 2025. https://wellcats.arizona.edu/grounding.

Havekost, Rachel. 2022. "Shadow Work Exercise." *Rachel Havekost* (blog), November 23. https://www.rachelhavekost.com/blog/shadow-work-exercise.

Heades, Rachael. n.d. "Signs You Should See a Private Therapist." Priory. Accessed July 12, 2025. https://www.priorygroup.com/blog/signs-you-should-see-a-therapist.

"The Healing Power of Art and Creativity." n.d. Salience Health. Accessed July 11, 2025. https://saliencehealth.com/news/the-healing-power-of-art-and-creativity/.

"Hermann Hesse." 2025. Encyclopedia Britannica, June 28. https://www.britannica.com/biography/Hermann-Hesse.

Hofmann, Stefan G., and Aleena C. Hay. 2018. "Rethinking Avoidance: Toward a Balanced Approach to Avoidance in Treating Anxiety Disorders." *Journal of Anxiety Disorders* 55 (April), 14–21. https://doi.org/10.1016/j.janxdis.2018.03.004.

Holland, Kimberly. 2022. "10 Defense Mechanisms: What Are They and How They Help Us Cope." *Healthline*, June 21. https://www.healthline.com/health/mental-health/defense-mechanisms.

"How to Celebrate Small Wins and Make Greater Progress." n.d. Feel More Connected. Accessed July 12, 2025. https://feelmoreconnected.com/how-to-celebrate-small-wins/.

"How to Integrate Your Shadow—The Dark Side Is Unrealized Potential." 2020. Academy of Ideas, February 27. https://academyofideas.com/2020/02/how-to-integrate-your-shadow/.

"How to Reduce Stress and Anxiety Through Movement and Mindfulness." 2025. Harvard Health, August 11. Accessed August 11, 2025. https://www.health.harvard.edu/mind-and-mood/how-to-reduce-stress-and-anxiety-through-movement-and-mindfulness.

"How to Understand Dreams and What They Reveal About Your Mental Health." 2024. Mindful Health Solutions, August 16. https://mindfulhealthsolutions.com/how-to-understand-dreams-and-what-they-reveal-about-your-mental-health/.

Hudson, Bren. 2025. "3-2-1 Shadow Work Process." Dr. Bren, July 4. https://www.drbren.com/blog/3-2-1-shadow-work-process.

Irven, Jasmine. n.d. "What Does It Mean to Set Intentions? (And How to Start Living More Intentionally.)" Sustainable Bliss. Accessed July 11, 2025. https://www.sustainablebliss.co.com/journal/setting-intentions.

Jeffrey, Scott. 2025a. "A Beginner's Guide to Jungian Shadow Work: How to Integrate Your Dark Side." Scott Jeffrey, January 25. https://scottjeffrey.com/shadow-work/.

Jeffrey, Scott. 2025b. "A Practical Guide to Jung's Active Imagination: How to Work with Archetypes." Scott Jeffrey, January 22. https://scottjeffrey.com/active-imagination/.

Johnson, Stephen. 2023. "Mini-personalities: Why Carl Jung Believed Your "Complexes" Lead Their Own Inner Lives." Big Think, September 8. https://bigthink.com/neuropsych/jung-autonomous-complexes-mini-personalities/.

"Jungian Archetypes: Self, Persona, Shadow, Anima/Animus." 2020. Eternalised, September 5. https://eternalisedofficial.com/2020/09/05/jungian-archetypes-explained/.

"The Jungian Shadow." 2015. The Society of Analytical Psychology, August 12. https://www.thesap.org.uk/articles-on-jungian-psychology-2/about-analysis-and-therapy/the-shadow/.

REFERENCES

Kamal, Maysara. 2024."What Is the Shadow According to Carl Jung?" The Collector, June 8. https://www.thecollector.com/what-is-shadow-according-to-carl-jung/.

King, Lucy. 2019. "Who Said Change Is the Only Constant in Life?" *Medium*, April 1. https://medium.com/mindset-matters/who-said-the-only-constant-in-life-is-change-233fd9e27b87.

Krüger, Rafael. 2024. "Carl Jung's Definitive Active Imagination Guide." Rafael Krüger, December 18. https://www.rafaelkruger.com/the-definitive-active-imagination-guide-by-carl-jung/.

Laisrén, Áine. 2023. "The Jungian Shadow Archetype and Dreams." Owlcation, November 26. https://owlcation.com/social-sciences/The-Shadow-Archetype-and-Shadow-Gold.

Lebow, Hilary I. 2021. "Trauma Denial: How to Recognize It and Why It Matters." *Psych Central*, November 12. https://psychcentral.com/blog/denial-of-trauma-signs.

Lepera, Nicole. 2021. "An Introduction to Reparenting." Maria Shriver, March 7. https://mariashriver.com/an-introduction-to-reparenting/.

Li, Jiayu, Weizhi Ma, Min Zhang, Pengyu Wang, Yiqun Liu, and Shaoping Ma. 2021. "Know Yourself: Physical and Psychological Self-Awareness with Lifelog." *Frontiers in Digital Health* 3 (August). https://doi.org/10.3389/fdgth.2021.676824.

Lindberg, Sara. 2018. "It's Not Me, It's You: Projection Explained in Human Terms." *Healthline*, September 15. https://www.healthline.com/health/projection-psychology.

LoBue, Vanessa, and Marissa Ogren. 2021. "How the Emotional Environment Shapes the Emotional Life of the Child." *Policy Insights from the Behavioral and Brain Sciences* 9, (1): 137–144. https://doi.org/10.1177/23727322211067264.

Lohret, Kim. n.d. "Understanding Resistance." Sage Hill Healing. Accessed July 11, 2025. https://www.sagehillhealing.com/understanding-resistance-and-shadow.

Lonngi, Gail. n.d. "The Jungian Shadow and Self-Acceptance." Texas A&M University at Galveston. Accessed July 11, 2025. https://www.tamug.edu/nautilus/articles/The%20Jungian%20Shadow%20and%20Self-Acceptance.html.

Lyons, Meg. 2021. "Being Your Authentic Self Is Easier Said Than Done but Worth It." *BetterUp* (blog), September 7. https://www.betterup.com/blog/authentic-self.

Manson, Mark. n.d. "How to Overcome Your Limiting Beliefs." Mark Manson. Accessed July 12, 2025. https://markmanson.net/limiting-beliefs.

McHale, Abby. n.d. "The Biggest Misconception of Shadow Work." Marigold Women. Accessed July 11, 2025. https://www.abbymchale.com/blog/the-biggest-misconception-of-shadow-work-protecting-our-joy.

McLaren, Karla. n.d. "Understanding and Befriending Anger." Karla McLaren. Accessed July 11, 2025. https://karlamclaren.com/understanding-and-befriending-anger/.

McMurrin, Morgan. 2024. "45 Carl Jung Quotes on Life, Wisdom and Perspective." *Parade*, May 6. https://parade.com/living/carl-jung-quotes.

McNally, Melanie A. 2024. "From Small Steps to Big Wins: The Importance of Celebrating." *Psychology Today*, June 12. https://www.psychologytoday.com/us/blog/empower-your-mind/202406/from-small-steps-to-big-wins-the-importance-of-celebrating.

"Mental Health Warning Signs and When to Ask for Help." n.d. The Jed Foundation. Accessed

July 12, 2025. https://jedfoundation.org/resource/mental-health-warning-signs-and-when-to-ask-for-help/.

"Mindfulness for Your Health." 2021. News in Health, June. Accessed August 11, 2025. https://newsinhealth.nih.gov/2021/06/mindfulness-your-health.

Mindful Staff. 2025. "What Is Mindfulness?" *Mindful*, May 15. https://www.mindful.org/what-is-mindfulness/.

Miranda, Leticia. n.d. "6 Steps to Breaking Your Limiting Beliefs." PushFar. Accessed July 12, 2025. https://www.pushfar.com/article/6-steps-to-breaking-your-limiting-beliefs/.

Molitor, Michelle. 2019. "Did You Know That Your Subconscious Mind Is Responsible for 95% of Your Brains Processing Power Beyond Your Conscious Awareness?" Michelle Molitor, December 9. https://michelemolitor.com/2019/12/09/the-95-5-rule/.

Moore, Jessica. 2018. "Solving Boundary Issues with Healthy Anger." *Medium*, July 27. https://medium.com/the-unlocked-heart/solving-boundary-issues-with-healthy-anger-b683e846f1de.

Myers Morgan, Meg. 2020. "Curiosity or Judgment: Flipping the Switch Changes Our Ability to Think, Lead and Understand." Meg Myers Morgan, March 14. https://www.megmyersmorgan.com/post/curiosity-or-judgment-flipping-the-switch-changes-our-ability-to-think-lead-and-understand.

Nash, Jo. 2018. "How to Set Healthy Boundaries & Build Positive Relationships." *PositivePsychology.com*, January 5. https://positivepsychology.com/great-self-care-setting-healthy-boundaries/.

Neff, Kristin. n.d. "What Is Self-Compassion?" Self-Compassion. Accessed July 11, 2025. https://self-compassion.org/what-is-self-compassion/.

Newman, Kira M. 2020. "How Journaling Can Help You in Hard Times." Greater Good, August 18. https://greatergood.berkeley.edu/article/item/how_journaling_can_help_you_in_hard_times.

Nicogossian, Claire. 2021. "What Are Shadow Emotions? How to Identify Yours." mindbodygreen, May 7. https://www.mindbodygreen.com/articles/shadow-emotions.

Nilsson, Stefan. 2022. "Quote of the Month: 'The Journey of a Thousand Miles Begins with One Step'." Hedge Funds Club, January 2. https://www.hedgefundsclub.com/archives/2887.

Nunez, Kirsten. 2023. "7 Simple Mindfulness Exercises You Can Easily Fit Into Your Day." *SELF*, April 27. https://www.self.com/story/best-mindfulness-exercises.

Oppong, Thomas. 2023. "Everything That Irritates You About Others Is the Secret to Self-Awareness." *Medium*, March 14. https://medium.com/personal-growth/carl-jung-every thing-that-irritates-you-about-others-can-create-immediate-self-awareness-58e2e8631110.

O'Rourke, Aisling. n.d. "Why You Should Be Sharing Your Success." The Communications Coach. Accessed July 12, 2025. https://thecommunicationscoach.ie/blog/2025/3/26/why-you-should-be-sharing-your-success.

Othon, Jack E. 2023. "Carl Jung and the Shadow: The Ultimate Guide to the Human Dark Side." HighExistence, January 11. https://www.highexistence.com/carl-jung-shadow-guide-unconscious/.

REFERENCES 139

Pal, Parneet, Carley Hauck, Elisha Goldstein, Kyra Bobinet, and Cara Bradley. 2024. "5 Simple Mindfulness Practices for Daily Life." *Mindful*, October 14. https://www.mindful.org/take-a-mindful-moment-5-simple-practices-for-daily-life/.

Peacock, Kelly. 2023. "7 Concrete Signs Your Shadow Work Is Actually Working." Collective World, November 8. https://collective.world/7-concrete-signs-your-shadow-work-is-actually-working/.

Perry, Elizabeth. 2024. "75 Shadow Work Prompts for Self-Discovery and Acceptance." *BetterUp* (blog), February 28. https://www.betterup.com/blog/shadow-work-prompts.

Pietrangelo, Ann. 2023. "The Effects of Stress on Your Body." *Healthline*, March 21. https://www.healthline.com/health/stress/effects-on-body.

"The Power of Setting Intentions & How to Set Mindful Ones." 2024. Calm, February 13. https://www.calm.com/blog/setting-intentions.

Rankin, Lissa. n.d. "How Do We Stop Projecting & Start Owning Our Mistakes?" Lissa Rankin. Accessed July 11, 2025. https://lissarankin.com/how-do-we-stop-projecting-start-owning-our-mistakes/.

Raveling, Barb. 2012. "9 Questions to Ask Before You Start People Pleasing." *Barb Raveling* (blog), October 1. https://barbraveling.com/living-up-to-expectations/.

Raypole, Crystal. 2024. "What to Know About Repressed Emotions." *Healthline*, October 25. https://www.healthline.com/health/repressed-emotions.

Rees, Sarah D. n.d. "Soothing Safe Place Imagery for Wellbeing." Sarah D Rees. Accessed July 11, 2025. https://sarahdrees.co.uk/soothing-safe-place-imagery-an-effective-tool-in-therapy/.

Reid, Sheldon. 2025. "Setting Healthy Boundaries in Relationships." HelpGuide, March 13. https://www.helpguide.org/relationships/social-connection/setting-healthy-boundaries-in-relationships.

Rennell, Frances. 2024. "Inner Sanctuary." Frances Rennell, November 9. https://creatingmindfullives.com.au/inner-sanctuary/.

Rinaldi, Joe. 2018. "Consistency Over Intensity." *Joe Rinaldi* (blog), March 7. https://joerinaldi.blog/2018/03/07/consistency-over-intensity/.

Rivera, Quinn. n.d. "Why You Need Consistency Instead of Intensity." Humbled Daily. Accessed July 12, 2025. https://www.humbleddaily.com/blogs/news/why-you-need-consistency-instead-of-intensity.

Roache, Rebecca. 2022. "How to Change Your Self-limiting Beliefs." *Psyche*, October 19. https://psyche.co/guides/how-philosophy-can-help-change-the-beliefs-that-hold-you-back.

Roberts, Emily. n.d. "The Importance of Self-Compassion." Hartstein Psychological Services. Accessed July 11, 2025. https://hartsteinpsychological.com/importance-self-compassion.

Roberts, Kim. 2023. "3 Steps to Finding Inner Sanctuary (in an Unsafe World)." *Medium*, November 7. https://medium.com/@KimRoberts108/finding-inner-sanctuary-6a40710391d1.

Robinson, Lawrence, Melinda Smith, and Jeanne Segal. 2025. "Emotional and Psychological

Trauma." HelpGuide.org, May 20. https://www.helpguide.org/mental-health/ptsd-trauma/coping-with-emotional-and-psychological-trauma.

Rothstein, Lori, and Denise Stromme. n.d. "Celebrate the Small Stuff." Extension at the University of Minnesota. Accessed July 12, 2025. https://extension.umn.edu/two-you-video-series/celebrate-small-stuff.

SAMHSA. 2014. "Understanding the Impact of Trauma," in *Trauma-Informed Care in Behavioral Health Services*. National Center for Biotechnology Information. https://www.ncbi.nlm.nih.gov/books/NBK207191/.

Sargeant, Kristan. n.d. "Getting to Know Your Shadow." The Tools. Accessed July 11, 2025. https://www.thetoolsbook.com/blog/getting-to-know-your-shadow.

Sciandra, Francesca. n.d. "30 Journal Prompts to Explore Your Creativity, Desires, and Passions." *Francesca Sciandra* (blog). Accessed July 11, 2025. https://francescasciandra.com/blog/30-journal-prompts-to-explore-your-creativity-desires-and-passions.

Serebrennikova, Natalia. n.d. "The Shadow." International Association of Analytical Psychology. Accessed July 11, 2025. https://iaap.org/jung-analytical-psychology/short-articles-on-analytical-psychology/the-shadow/.

"The Shadow—Carl Jung's Warning to the World." 2021. Eternalised, October 1. https://eternalisedofficial.com/2021/10/01/the-shadow-carl-jung-warning/.

"Shadow Self Quotes: Thought-Provoking Sayings About Inner Darkness." 2023. SOLANCHA, February 27. https://solancha.com/shadow-self-quotes-thought-provoking-sayings-about-inner-darkness/.

"Shadow Work Mythbusting." n.d. *Compassionate Talk Therapy* (blog). Accessed July 11, 2025. https://www.compassionatetalktherapy.com/about-1-1-1-2-1-1-1-1-1-1.

"Shadow Work, the Archetypes and Defense Mechanisms." n.d. Myndworx. Accessed July 12, 2025. https://myndworx.net/shadow-work-the-archetypes-and-defense-mechanisms-explained/.

Shaheen, Keila, and Connie Zweig. 2024. "3 Myths About Shadow Work Debunked." Shadow Work to Expand Awareness, October 25. https://www.shadowworkawareness.com/p/3-myths-about-shadow-work-debunked.

Sinclair, Amelia. n.d. "Journey Into the Psyche: The Life and Works of Carl Jung." Achology. Accessed July 11, 2025. https://achology.com/psychology/the-life-and-works-of-carl-jung/.

Smith, Sydney. 2022. "How to Release Fear in 4 Steps." *Adventuring with Poseidon* (blog), March 3. https://www.adventuringwithposeidon.com/blog/how-to-release-fear-in-4-steps.

Solis-Moreira, Jocelyn. 2024. "How Long Does It Really Take to Form a Habit?" *Scientific American*, January 24. https://www.scientificamerican.com/article/how-long-does-it-really-take-to-form-a-habit/.

Stockwell, Bernadette. 2022. "How to Turn Negative Emotions Into Inspiration for Action." *Psychology Today*, December 31. https://www.psychologytoday.com/us/blog/the-naked-creative/202212/how-to-turn-negative-emotions-into-inspiration-for-action.

Subramaniam, Aditi. 2022. "The Positives of Negative Emotion." *Psychology Today*, August 4.

https://www.psychologytoday.com/us/blog/parenting-neuroscience-perspective/202208/the-positives-negative-emotion.

Sutton, Jeremy. 2022. "7 Best Grounding Tools and Techniques to Manage Anxiety." *Positive-Psychology.com*, January 2. https://positivepsychology.com/grounding-tools-techniques/.

Swerdloff, Michael. 2024. "9 Signs You've Done Your Shadow Work." Michael Swerdloff, March 31. https://www.michaelswerdloff.com/signs-shadow-work/.

"Tap Into Your Dark Side with Shadow Work." 2023. Cleveland Clinic, August 1. https://health.clevelandclinic.org/shadow-work.

Tartakovsky, Margarita. 2014. "25 Questions for Cultivating Self-Compassion." *Psych Central*, October 24. https://psychcentral.com/blog/25-questions-for-cultivating-self-compassion#1.

"10 Mindfulness Questions to Help You Check In with Yourself." 2024. Calm, January 16. https://www.calm.com/blog/check-in-with-yourself.

"13 Grounding Techniques To Help Calm Anxiety." 2024. Cleveland Clinic, November 25. Accessed August 11, 2025. https://health.clevelandclinic.org/grounding-techniques.

"35 Small Wins to Celebrate This Week." 2021. *Ink and Volt* (blog), December 29. https://inkandvolt.com/blogs/articles/35-small-wins-to-celebrate-this-week.

"The 3-2-1 Process." n.d. Integral Life. Accessed July 11, 2025. https://integrallife.com/the-3-2-1-shadow-process/.

"3-2-1 Process for the Shadow." n.d. Bhavana Learning Group. Accessed July 12, 2025. https://bhavanalearninggroup.com/wp-content/uploads/321-Process-for-the-Shadow.pdf.

"Tips for Crafting an At-Home Meditation Sanctuary." 2020. Rituals, December 1. https://www.rituals.com/en-nl/mag-home-living-create-your-meditation-space-at-home.html.

Tolle, Eckhart. 2010. *The Power of Now: A Guide to Spiritual Enlightenment*. Novato: New World Library.

Toniolo, Jonathan. 2020. "Spiritual Bypassing: How Spirituality Sabotaged My Growth." HighExistence, January 31. https://www.highexistence.com/spiritual-bypassing-how-spirituality-sabotaged-my-growth/.

"Trauma Denial: What Is It and Why Does It Happen." 2024. Khiron, August 30. https://khironclinics.com/blog/trauma-denial-what-is-it-and-why-does-it-happen/.

Trovato, Egle. 2023. "How to Do Shadow Work with Art: A Guide." Mae, July 26. https://www.mae.community/magazine/how-to-do-shadow-work-with-art-a-guide.

Tumanishvili, George G. n.d. "Turning Negative Emotions Into Positive Motivation." International Institute of Time Management. Accessed July 12, 2025. https://time-management.org/turning-negative-emotions-into-positive-motivation/.

"The Ultimate Guide to Shadow Work Journaling." 2025. *Reflection* (blog), March 25. https://www.reflection.app/blog/the-ultimate-guide-to-shadow-work-journaling.

Valverde, Sara. n.d. "How to Clear the Emotional Clutter That Weighs You Down." *Tiny Buddha* (blog). Accessed July 11, 2025. https://tinybuddha.com/blog/how-to-clear-the-emotional-clutter-that-weighs-you-down/.

Veale, David, Eleanor Robins, Alex B. Thomson, and Paul Gilbert. 2023. "No Safety Without

Emotional Safety." *The Lancet Psychiatry* 10 (1): 65–70. https://doi.org/10.1016/s2215-0366(22)00373-x.

Villines, Zawn. 2023. "What Is Shadow Work? What to Know." *Medical News Today*, November 8. https://www.medicalnewstoday.com/articles/what-is-shadow-work.

Waschenfelder, Thomas. n.d. "The Other Side of Fear Is Preparation." Wealest. Accessed July 12, 2025. https://www.wealest.com/articles/fear.

Webb Wright, Kristen. 2023. "15 Ways to Cultivate Emotional Resilience." Day One, June 14. https://dayoneapp.com/blog/emotional-resilience/.

"What Is Mindfulness?" n.d. *Greater Good Magazine*. Accessed July 11, 2025. https://greatergood.berkeley.edu/topic/mindfulness/definition.

Wiginton, Keri. 2024. "What Is Shadow Work? How to Start and Benefits." WebMD, July 25. https://www.webmd.com/mental-health/shadow-work.

Wilber, Ken. 2000. *A Theory of Everything: An Integral Vision for Business, Politics, Science, and Spirituality*. Boulder: Shambhala Publications.

Williams, Jennifer A. n.d. "Inner Peace Requires You to Be Present with Self-Compassion." *Heartmanity* (blog). Accessed July 11, 2025. https://blog.heartmanity.com/inner-peace-requires-you-to-be-present-with-self-compassion.

Williams, Ruth. 2025. "Three Ways to Get in Touch with Your Shadow Self." *Psyche*, April 7. https://psyche.co/guides/three-ways-to-get-in-touch-with-your-shadow-self.

Wilson, Mitchell. 2023. "Active Imagination 101: Jungian Analyst Robert Johnson's 4-Step Practical Way to Reveal & Interact with Layers of Your Soul (That You Never Knew You Had) for Even Deeper Personal Growth." Top-Tier Mental Wealth, December 31. https://www.mitchellwilson.co/post/active-imagination-101-robert-johnsons-4-step-practical-way-to-reveal-interact-with-layers-of-your-soul.

Wisner, Wendy. 2023. "How to Express Jealousy in a Positive Way." *Verywell Mind*, December 5. https://www.verywellmind.com/healthy-ways-to-express-jealousy-in-relationships-5216590.

Wong, Albert. 2023. "Projection as Defense Mechanism & How to Work with It." Osomatopia, March 3. https://www.somatopia.com/blog/projection-as-defense-mechanism-how-to-work-with-it.

Woolfe, Sam. 2016. "Carl Jung and Hermann Hesse Explain Why Other People Irritate Us." Sam Woolfe, November 3. https://www.samwoolfe.com/2016/11/carl-jung-and-hermann-hesse-explain-why.html.

Wooll, Maggie. 2022. "Don't Let Limiting Beliefs Hold You Back. Learn to Overcome Yours." *BetterUp* (blog), July 19. https://www.betterup.com/blog/what-are-limiting-beliefs.

Yaw, Naomi. n.d. "3 Questions Every People-Pleaser Should Ask Before Making a Decision." *Tiny Buddha* (blog). Accessed July 12, 2025. https://tinybuddha.com/blog/3-questions-every-people-pleaser-should-ask-before-making-a-decision/.

"Your Future Self (My Favorite Visualization)." n.d. Wholehearted Coaching. Accessed July 12, 2025. https://www.wholehearted-coaching.com/podcast/future-self-visualization.

Zaltman, Gerald. 2003. "The Subconscious Mind of the Consumer (and How to Reach It)." Harvard Business School, January 13. https://www.library.hbs.edu/working-knowledge/the-subconscious-mind-of-the-consumer-and-how-to-reach-it.

Made in the USA
Coppell, TX
22 February 2026